A Noble Calling

A Noble Calling

Devotions and Esssays for Business Professionals

DAVID WESLEY WHITLOCK
GORDON DUTILE
EDITORS

FOREWORD BY BOB R. AGEE

Featuring Contributions From:
Troy Bethards, Bart C. Craytor, Ronda O. Credille,
Susan Debauche, Timothy DeClue, Gordon Dutile,
David Dyson, Barry Ellis, T. David Gordon,
Jeffrey M. Herbener, Julie Huntley, Sharon Johnson,
Jeff Kimball, Phil V. Lewis, Rodger W. Minatra,
R. Stanton Norman, Rodney Allen Oglesby, Rodney Reeves,
Shawn Ritenour, James R. Russell, Galen Smith,
Tom Stevens, David B. Whitlock,
David Wesley Whitlock and Marshal Wright

WIPF & STOCK · Eugene, Oregon

A NOBLE CALLING

Devotions and Esssays for Busniess Professionals

Copyright © David Wesley Whitlock & Gordon Dutile, 2008. All rights reserved. Except for brief quotations in critical publications or reviews, no part of this book may be reproduced in any manner without prior written permission from the publisher. Write: Permissions, Wipf and Stock, 199 W. 8th Ave., Suite 3, Eugene, OR 97401.

ISBN 13: 978-1-55635-536-3

Manufactured in the U.S.A.

All rights reserved. No part of this publication may be reproduced or utilized in any form or by any means, electronic or mechanical, including photocopying, microfilm and recording or by any information storage and retrieval system, without the written permission of the publisher. Printed in the United States of America.

Unless otherwise noted, all Scripture quotations are taken from the Holman Christian Standard Bible©, 1999, 2000, 2002, 2003 by Holman Bible Publishers. Used by permission. Holman Christian Standard Bible©, Holman CSB©, and HCSB© are federally registered trademarks of Holman Bible Publishers.

Scripture quotations "NASB" are taken from the New American Standard Bible©, 1960,1962,1963,1968,1971,1972,1973,1975,1977,1995 by The Lockman Foundation. Used by permission.

Scripture quotations marked "NKJV" are taken from The New King James Version© / Thomas Nelson Publishers, Nashville : Thomas Nelson Publishers 1982. Used by permission. All rights reserved.

Scripture quotations marked "NIV" are taken from Holy Bible, New International Version© 1973, 1978, 1984 by International Bible Society. Used by permission of Zondervan Publishing House." All rights reserved. The "NIV©" and "New International Version©" trademarks are registered in the United States Patent and Trademark Office by International Bible Society. Use of either trademark requires the permission of International Bible Society.

Scripture quotations marked "NRSV" are taken from New Revised Standard Version Bible©, 1989 National Council of the Churches of Christ in the United States of America. Used by permission. All rights reserved.

Scripture quotations marked "NLT" are taken from the Holy Bible, New Living Translation©, 1996. Used by permission of Tyndale House Publishers, Inc., Wheaton, Illinois 60189. All rights reserved.

Scripture quotations marked "ESV" are from The Holy Bible, English Standard Version©, 2001 by Crossway Bibles, a publishing ministry of Good News Publishers. Used by permission. All rights reserved

Scripture quotations marked "KJV" are taken from the Holy Bible, King James Version©, Cambridge, 1769.

This book is dedicated to business leaders and professionals who serve as ambassadors for Christ as they fulfill the roles God has designed for them.

Keep the faith so that when your work is completed you will hear the Master tell you, "Well done, good and faithful servant."

Contents

Acknowledgments / xi
Foreword / xiii
Introduction / xv

Part I: A Matter of Character

1: Integrity
The Essence of Integrity
—*Gordon Dutile* / 5

2: Service
Service: Putting Others First,
—*Ronda O. Credille* / 11

3: Respect
All I'm Asking For
—*Susan Debauche* / 19

4: Charity
Charity: Preserving the Dignity of Work,
—*David Wesley Whitlock* / 25

5: Faithfulness
A Picture of Faithfulness
—*Rodney Reeves* / 33

6: Truthfulness
The Truth Shall Set You Free
—*Bart C. Craytor* / 39

7: Humility
Humility: Attitude and Action
—*Rodger W. Minatra* / 45

8: Perseverance
What Keeps You Going?
—*R. Stanton Norman* / 51

Part II: A Matter of Worldview

9: Marketing, Management and Technology

Redeemed Marketing
 —*Julie Huntley and David Dyson* / 65

Under New Management
 —*Ronda O. Credille* / 69

Of Heroes and Managers
 —*Phil V. Lewis* / 79

Talents and Technology
 —*Timothy DeClue and Jeffrey Kimball* / 84

God's Mandate and Entrepreneurship
 —*T. David Gordon and Jeffrey M. Herbener* / 90

10: Competition, Success and Ethics

Perspectives on Competition,
 —*Sharon G. Johnson and Galen Smith* / 103

Defining Success
 —*Rodger W. Minatra* / 110

Success: The Never-Ending Journey
 —*David B. Whitlock* / 113

He Was a Successful Man
 —*David Wesley Whitlock* / 124

An Ethics Primer
 —*Troy Bethards* / 127

Ethics and the Marketplace
 —*Bart C. Craytor* / 131

11: Accounting, Finance and Economics

A Biblical Basis for Accounting
 —*Rodney Allen Oglesby* / 139

Finance: Toward a Biblical Worldview
 —*Tom D. Stevens* / 143

Judeo-Christian Influences on Socioeconomics
 —*Marshal H Wright and James R. Russell* / 150

Economics: A Biblical Perspective
 —*Shawn Ritenour* / 157

12: Leadership and Motivation

Style, Power and the Servant Leader
—*David Wesley Whitlock* / 171

Free to Serve
—*Tom D. Stevens* / 175

Motivation: A New Model
—*David Wesley Whitlock* / 179

Part III: A Matter of Faith

13: Putting it into Practice

The Necessity of a Biblical Christian Worldview
—*Gordon Dutile* / 187

A Life of Faith: Lessons from Joseph
—*David Wesley Whitlock* / 191

Epilogue / 199

Appendix / 203

Usury and Interest: A Christian Perspective
—*David Wesley Whitlock* / 205

Capital Rationing and the Fall
—*R. Barry Ellis* / 209

Acknowledgments

This project is the result of collaboration by numerous colleagues and thinkers dedicated to promoting the concept of applying a biblical worldview to the practice of business. In addition to chapter contributors, the following individuals are acknowledged for their suggestions, assistance, and encouragement:

Rhonda Agee
Sharla Bailey
Wayne Clark
James Cain
Judy Dutile
Vickie Shamp Ellis
Marinell Erven
Shelly Francka
C. Henry Gold
Daniel Neumann
C. Pat Taylor
Dana Leigh Whitlock

Special thanks are expressed to Susan Debauche for her work as a copyeditor for this project and to Tina Campbell Owens, Carrie Wolcott, and Scarlettah Schaefer at Wipf and Stock Publishers for their assistance. Of course this project would not have been possible without the unselfish contributions of each author.

For their participation, the following contributors are recognized:

Bob R. Agee
Troy Bethards
Bart C. Craytor
Ronda O. Credille
Susan Debauche
Timothy DeClue
Gordon Dutile
David Dyson
R. Barry Ellis
T. David Gordon
Jeffrey M. Herbener
Julie Huntley
Sharon G. Johnson
Jeffrey Kimball
Phil V. Lewis
Rodger W. Minatra
R. Stanton Norman
Rodney Oglesby
Rodney Reeves
Shawn Ritenour
James R. Russell
Galen Smith
Tom D. Stevens
David B. Whitlock
David Wesley Whitlock
Marshal Wright

All royalties generated from the sale of this book are donated to charitable causes.

Foreword

THE WORLD of work seems to get more challenging every day as pressures to achieve and succeed make daily demands upon a person. It's not unusual to begin to feel as though stresses and issues are being piled higher than our heads. There are a number of things my fifty years as a working professional have taught me. One prominent impression continues to grow: I am not always adequate for the demands and challenges. I need a source of help from beyond myself to guide me and to provide me with insights and understandings that will enable me to make wise decisions and choose good courses of action.

This book of devotionals is designed for the person who faces the demands and challenges of the day to day workplace. Each contributor has learned that guidance from above helps in dealing with issues and in searching for answers to daily perplexities. Drs. Whitlock and Dutile have spent their careers helping young men and women find the divine guidance needed to make good career choices. The insights provided in this book seek to help in making application to spiritual truths to the challenges we face every day.

Among life's greatest truths has been the reality that I don't have to face life alone and my knowledge and wisdom do not have to be sufficient for me to find the right way to do the right things. Knowing that God cares about every facet of my life and is deeply interested in who I am and in the way I do business give me a keen sense of accountability to Him. Knowing also, that God has been involved in where I am and what I'm doing and has planted me in my workplace to be a "Kingdom Outpost" in His world, has turned every place I've worked into a platform for witness and ministry. Countless times I've discovered new paths, new strategies, new creativity, and additional courage because His hand was on me and my place of work.

I would admonish the reader to make this a daily devotional guide. Dip often into the well of Biblical insights contained in this volume. Don't be afraid to apply spiritual truth to your daily tasks. God is indeed both worthy of our devotion and adequate for the demands of our days.

Bob R. Agee, PhD
President Emeritus
Oklahoma Baptist University

Introduction

A Psalm 15 Leader

For years, students and professionals alike have expressed concern over their chosen field of study or choice of profession. For many, this struggle has often centered on a false dichotomy that lives on in spite of the efforts of the sixteenth century reformers who, among other critical issues of doctrine and ecclesiology, advanced the perspective of equality before God between the clergy and the laity.

Too often, individuals who have been called to practice their gifts and talents in the field of business and professional life sense that to serve God they ought to be doing something more directly involved with the church. Many successful business leaders, upon coming to faith in Christ or upon renewing their interest in God's Word, struggle with whether or not they should enter vocational ministry. Certainly, God calls some from among the professions into such vocations, but I am convinced that many simply haven't realized the full potential of where God has placed them.

One of my mentors in higher education is Dr. Bob Agee. Dr. Agee, years ago seemed to sense that I was struggling with this very issue, even though I had not revealed my thoughts to him. He looked at me intently and spoke about the stewardship of experience. He explained that God desires to use everything I have experienced including my education and work life. Everything. While I suppose that reality should have been self-evident, Dr. Agee's advice was like a thunderbolt. God desires to use everything. There is great freedom in realizing that the calling to business and professional life is every bit as valid and significant to Kingdom work as the calling to vocational ministry.

In the years since then, I have become increasingly convinced of this truth and of the fact that God's people who are assigned to duties in corporate board rooms, offices, on sales forces, in entrepreneurial ventures, as members of research and development teams, are among His most effective servants. These individuals who are active in the marketplace are among His most treasured ministers and have the potential to have a wider impact and larger influence than most full-time pastors and ministers.

Introduction

Likewise, these professionals have a capacity for great harm to the church and the cause of Christ if while making claims of belief, their actions prove inconsistent with what God's Word teaches—if their walk doesn't match their talk.

As a lifelong educator, I have sought to teach students and encourage fellow believers in the marketplace to walk the walk, to be consistent, believing that business and professional life holds great potential for good for those who trust in God. I am convinced that what Dr. Agee instilled in me so many years ago is true. God wants to use you, right now, where you are; and He desires to sanctify all of your experiences for His purposes. What God desires for His followers is that they walk uprightly, speak truth, deal fairly, honor Him, keep their word, and reach out to others—that they love the Lord with all their heart, mind, and strength, and love others as themselves.

Psalm 15 summarizes the kind of person who dwells with God, and its words ought to characterize the follower of God who represents Him in the conduct of business.

> The Character of Those Who May Dwell with the LORD
> LORD, who may abide in Your tabernacle?
> Who may dwell in Your holy hill?
> He who walks uprightly,
> And works righteousness,
> And speaks the truth in his heart;
> He who does not backbite with his tongue,
> Nor does evil to his neighbor,
> Nor does he take up a reproach against his friend;
> In whose eyes a vile person is despised,
> But he honors those who fear the LORD;
> He who swears to his own hurt and does not change;
> He who does not put out his money at usury[1],
> Nor does he take a bribe against the innocent.
> He who does these things shall never be moved
> (Ps. 15: 1–5 NKJV)

It is not an exaggeration to say that such a person is not only a good ambassador for Christ, but also that such a person is pleasing to God. For those called into vocations involving entrepreneurial ventures, professional careers, and positions in business, take heed. Your calling is noble. Conduct yourself, therefore, with consistency and purpose, working as unto the Lord. Determine to honor God in all your dealings. Dedicate yourself

---

1. For thoughts on usury and interest, see *Psalm 15 and Usury* in the Appendix.

Introduction

to being a *Psalm 15 professional*—a *Psalm 15 leader*. This book was originally conceived for the purpose of compiling devotions on the character traits described in Psalm 15 and was then expanded to include a broad overview of several functional areas in business and professional life.

A Noble Calling is a collection of essays and devotions, presented in three parts. *Part One: A Matter of Character* contains devotions on the character traits that are typified by the answer to Psalm 15's introduction/title and question: "The character of those who may dwell with the LORD. LORD, who may abide in Your tabernacle? Who may dwell in Your holy hill?" *Part Two: A Matter of Worldview* contains chapters devoted to essays and devotions that cause the reader to consider about how their calling can be consecrated for God's purposes. The desire of the contributors to this book is that you will be impressed to free yourself from a false dichotomy that pits ministry over and against the conduct of business and professional life. The hope of the contributors to this collection of devotions and essays is that you will be liberated from a mindset that artificially separates our Christian life and spirituality from our professional life. Our goal is to help professionals to quit thinking in terms of church life and work life as two different spheres.

Finally, *Part Three: A Matter of Faith* is simply a challenge to operate with the knowledge that the Lord is Lord of all in your life, or else He is the Lord of nothing in your life. Part Three is a challenge to live a life that clearly evidences your own faith in Christ, your own commitment to walk in a manner worthy of the gospel of Christ. As the apostle Paul wrote in Philippians "Just one thing: live your life in a manner worthy of the gospel of Christ. Then, whether I come and see you or am absent, I will hear about you that you are standing firm in one spirit, with one mind, working side by side for the faith of the gospel" (Phil. 1:27). Each of us, regardless of our vocational calling should strive to live a life worthy of the name *Christian*.

Be encouraged! God wants to use you where you are. He wants to sanctify all of what you have learned and experienced. You have great potential in the Kingdom! Your colleagues are observing you and your conduct, testing your actions by what is taught in God's Word. My co-editor and I pray that you will be found faithful, consistent, and the kind of person described in Psalm 15.

DWW

Part I
A Matter of Character

Devotions on Character

- ❧ Integrity
- ❧ Service
- ❧ Respect
- ❧ Charity
- ❧ Faithfulness
- ❧ Truthfulness
- ❧ Humility
- ❧ Perseverance

1

Integrity

"But let your word 'yes' be 'yes' and your 'no' be 'no.'
Anything more than this is from the evil one."
—Matt. 5:37

"He stores up success for the upright;
He is a shield for those who live with integrity."
—Prov. 2:7

"Better is the poor who walks in integrity
than he who is crooked though he be rich."
—Prov. 28:6 NASB

The Essence of Integrity

Gordon Dutile

The Hebrew concept translated by the English word "integrity" communicates the ideas of completeness, soundness, wholeness, and purity. Even after Job had lost his family and all of his possessions, God said to Satan, "Have you considered My servant Job? For there is no one like him on the earth, a blameless and upright man fearing God and turning away from evil. And he still holds fast his integrity, although you incited Me against him, to ruin him without cause" (Job 2:3, NASB). It is the overarching essence of character. A person of integrity reflects the qualities of life that commend themselves to others. Integrity demonstrates strength of character that enables the individual, regardless of circumstances, to live out what Romans 8:28 teaches. "And we know that God causes all things to work together for good to those who love God, to those who are called according to His purpose" (Rom. 8:28 NASB).

Look at Joseph who as a young man, probably a teenager, was sold by his jealous brothers into slavery. Many would have used his terrible circumstances as an excuse to give up and have a pity party. Instead Joseph revealed a rock-solid confidence in the sovereign God of Israel to guide, protect, and provide for him. He found himself in an Egyptian home and exhibited such responsibility that he ended up as the manager of the household. When he resisted the sexual advances of his master's wife, she falsely accused him of attempted rape. He wound up in prison during which time he befriended the baker and cupbearer of the Egyptian Pharaoh, helping each of them interpret his dream. His only request of them was that when they got out, they would not forget him; however, he was forgotten. Ultimately, Joseph was remembered and became second in command in Egypt. He not only helped to save the Egyptian people during a difficult famine, but he became the instrument in the deliverance of his father's family including his brothers who had sold him into slavery. His actions and responses during this saga were a demonstration of unquestionable integrity. He opted to exhibit self-control when he had the opportunity to fulfill self-gratification. He revealed trust in God when he could have yielded to despair and self-pity. He exercised forgiveness and compassion when he could have reacted in a spirit of anger and vengeance.

Proverbs has the following to say about the person of integrity. "He stores up sound wisdom for the upright; He is a shield to those who walk in integrity" (Prov. 2:7 NASB). "He who walks in integrity walks securely, but he who perverts his ways will be found out" (Prov. 10:9 NASB). "The integrity of the upright will guide them, but the crookedness of the treacherous will destroy them" (Prov. 11:3 NASB). "A righteous man who walks in integrity—how blessed are his sons after him" (Prov. 20:7 NASB). "Better is the poor who walks in integrity than he who is crooked though he be rich" (Prov. 28:6 NASB).

The Greek word used in the New Testament that I think most closely communicates integrity is a word that is often translated as pure or sincere. The root idea of the word is unalloyed. This Greek word is a combination of two words, sun and to judge. It was used at times to describe the picture of a buyer examining a piece of glassware in the sunlight to determine if the merchant was attempting to cover a crack in the item by filling it with wax.

A Christian life characterized by integrity is able to withstand the scrutiny of a skeptical world. When placed under such intense examination, it reveals itself as unmixed, unalloyed, pure, and sincere. This quality is exhibited in the life of one who has a personal relationship with the Lord Jesus. That relationship is constantly growing and is empowered by the Holy Spirit. The person of integrity is quick to realize that pride goes before a fall, and therefore humbly recognizes her or his total dependence on the grace and mercy of God.

It is important to focus on the concept of unmixed, unalloyed, and pure. It is not an accident or coincidence that the first commandment is, "You shall have no other gods before Me" (Exod. 20:3 NASB). In response to the question as to which commandment is the most important, Jesus said it this way, "The foremost is, 'Hear, O Israel; the Lord our God is one Lord; and you shall love the Lord your God with all your heart, and with all your soul, and with all your mind, and with all your strength'" (Mark 12:29–30 NASB). To be a person of biblical integrity, he or she must be single-minded. There can not be any split allegiance. In teaching the Bible, I have often noted that the appropriate approach to the Christian life is to be sold out to God. If our allegiance and commitment are to God and God alone, all other aspects or areas of life will be managed and cared for appropriately. If Jesus is Lord of all, He will guide the believer to do the right thing in every relationship and situation. We will not have to make a list of whom or what comes next. The Lord will lead us to do what is right and best. Paul's prayer for the Philippians was, "And this I pray, that your love may abound still more and more in real knowledge and all discernment, so that you may approve the things that are excellent, in order to be sincere and blameless until the day of Christ" (Phil. 1:9–10 NASB). The Christian whose life is characterized by integrity is able to distinguish not only that which is good but that which is most excellent, that which is best.

I shall never forget the example set for me by a dear saint who was a member of the church that I served as associate pastor while I was in seminary. She worked for the government in a clerical area. She told me that when she was at her job, she did not take time away from her responsibilities to witness or to read her Bible. Her commitment to God and His rule in her life led her to believe that she was to be the best employee possible. To use "company time" to witness when she was being paid to work was an act of dishonesty and would be hurtful to her testimony as a Christian. When she was on her allowed breaks during the day, she actively looked for the opportunity to share her faith. Her focus in life was to be what God wanted her to be. She was single-minded in her purpose, unmixed in her motives. That enabled her to see all of life as a means to serve God. That commitment made her a better church member, wife, mother, friend and employee. She exemplified to me what Paul meant when the Spirit led him to write, "Whether, then, you eat or drink or whatever you do, do all to the glory of God" (1 Cor. 10:31 NASB).

In summary, Christian integrity does not mean that the individual has reached a state of flawless perfection. It is, however, a virtue that results from the believer maturing in the image of Christ and growing more and more aware of her or his absolute dependence on the power provided by God. The textbook for integrity is the Word of God. Timothy received the following admonition from his mentor: "Be diligent to present yourself approved to God as a workman who does not need to be ashamed, handling accurately the word of truth" (1 Tim. 2:15 NASB). The Christian who exhibits this quality will always exclaim along with the apostle Paul, "But by the grace of God I am what I am, and His grace toward me did not prove vain." (1 Cor. 15:10a NASB).

Gordon Dutile is the Provost at Southwest Baptist University where he also served for many years as a professor of Greek. He holds a BS from Louisiana Tech University, and the MDiv and PhD from Southwestern Baptist Theological Seminary.

2

Service

"Serve the LORD with gladness;
come before Him with joyful songs."
—Ps. 100:2

"But Jesus called them over and said, 'You know that the rulers of the Gentiles dominate them, and the men of high position exercise power over them. It must not be like that among you. On the contrary, whoever wants to become great among you must be your servant, and whoever wants to be first among you must be your slave; just as the Son of Man did not come to be served, but to serve, and to give His life—a ransom for many.'"
—Matt. 20:25–28

"Let us not become weary in doing good, for at the proper time we will reap a harvest if we do not give up."
—Gal. 6:9 NIV

"It is not fitting, when one is in God's service,
to have a gloomy face or a chilling look."
—Saint Francis of Assisi

Service

Ronda O. Credille

THE SNOWFLAKES were so large that I used an umbrella as I carefully walked through the parking lot to my office building early one morning. Though the snow had been falling for little more than an hour, the parking lot was already covered with a thick blanket of white. *The physical plant crew probably hasn't had time to shovel the sidewalk either,* I thought to myself. The sidewalk slopes downward from the parking lot to the building and can become slippery during winter precipitation. But to my surprise and relief, the sidewalk was clear.

Later in the day I learned that the housekeeper for the building, Chong "Lena" Campbell, a petite native of Korea, had shoveled the sidewalk before she began her regularly assigned duties indoors; a fellow faculty member had spotted her in action. She knew the physical plant crew would not be able to get to our sidewalk before college students and faculty members arrived for early morning classes. So she took the task upon herself. Lena rendered a tremendous service to a hundred or so members of the university family, yet if she had not been caught in the act, no one would have known that she was our benefactor.

What is Service? The word *service* is a familiar term in the American vocabulary. Approximately 80% of the U.S. economy is service-based.[1] Occupations in the service sector, specifically in the health and computer programming industries, are forecasted to provide most of the new jobs created in the near future.[2] Businesses often tout their customer service in advertisements. Not coincidentally, a survey conducted by the Mystery Shopping Providers Association indicated that 93% of the 3,500 people

---

1. "Service sector extends advance but signals pace might slow." (February 6, 2007). *The Wall Street Journal*, A2. Retrieved March 24, 2007 from http://online.wsj.com/public.

2. "High-Paying Careers of the Next Two Decades." *Futurist*, Jan/Feb 2007 Supplement, Vol. 41, p. 7. *Business Source Premier*. March 24, 2007. http://search.ebscohost.com.

surveyed considered "employee courtesy and employee knowledge" to be "the most important elements" of a shopping experience.[3]

With so much emphasis on service, it would seem logical to have people lining up for positions as servants. Yet it is rare to hear the latter mentioned outside of religious circles. What image comes to mind when you think of the word servant? A French maid? A British butler? Servant often connotes someone who performs household tasks, perhaps of a menial nature.

One of the greatest leaders of the New Testament church was the apostle Paul, yet he referred to himself as, "Paul, a servant of God," (Titus 1:1 NIV) and "Paul, a servant of Christ Jesus" (Rom. 1:1 NIV). One might wonder if his humility stemmed from the fact that his actions had led to the martyrdom of many Christians. That explanation is unlikely. Paul instructed believers to, "*Serve* one another in love" (Gal. 5:13 NIV italics added) and to serve employers (literally, masters) "wholeheartedly, as if you were serving the Lord" (Eph. 6:7 NIV).

Charles Swindoll states that God's main objective for His children is to build into them "the same serving and giving qualities" that "made Jesus distinct from all others in His day."[4] Swindoll acknowledges that this is "a lifestyle totally at variance with the world system."[5] Human nature is concerned with not only self-preservation, but self-advancement. No wonder some of the people of Thessalonica accused Paul and Silas of "upset[ting] the world" with their teachings (Acts 17:6 NIV)! John Beckett notes that the early disciples were modeling Christ because they "understood the joy of sacrifice and the reward in serving."[6] Following the example of their Lord, they "extend[ed] themselves on the behalf of others."[7] His phrase encapsulates the idea of servanthood.

The late Bob Briner, former president of ProServ Television, observed, "The conventional wisdom [in business] is that to be number one, you must take care of number one."[8] Briner contradicted this assumption by referring to Jesus' declaration in Matthew 23:11: "The greatest among you will be your servant." Briner explained, "This kind of servanthood

---

3. "No mystery here: Courtesy counts," *Convenience Store News*, 42(4) (2006), 8.

4. Swindoll, C. R., *Improving Your Serve: The Art of Unselfish Living* (Waco, Texas: Word, Inc. 1981), 18.

5. Ibid., p. 98.

6. Beckett, J. D., *Loving Monday*. (Downers Grove, Illinois: InterVarsity Press 1998), 117.

7. Ibid., 117.

8. Briner, B., *The Management Methods of Jesus: Ancient Wisdom for Modern Business*. (Nashville, Tennessee: Thomas Nelson, Inc. 1996), 57.

require[s] an attitude that asks, "How can I best take care of the needs of my employees and customers in the context of a growing, thriving business?"[9]

What Are the Characteristics of a Servant? Swindoll calls the Beatitudes (Matt. 5:1–12) "the most descriptive word-portrait of a servant ever recorded."[10] Swindoll goes on to say that Jesus "has described our calling by explaining our role as:

Poor in spirit
Mourning
Gentle
Hungering and thirsting for righteousness
Merciful
Pure in heart
Peacemakers
Persecuted[11]

Beckett identifies two prerequisites to genuine servanthood: sincere motivations and a biblical foundation.[12] The Apostle Paul warned Timothy about people "who think that godliness is a means to financial gain" (1 Tim. 6:5 NIV). Those who serve for the purpose of being noticed or repaid are not true servants; they merely view acts of service as a means of personal gain. Dr. John Wheeler, a college professor and a preaching elder at Wellspring Fellowship in Bolivar, reminds our congregation regularly that we are to minister to people at the point of their need—not at the point of our need to minister. Paul declared that, "we are God's workmanship, created in Christ Jesus to do good works, which God prepared in advance for us to do" (Eph. 2:10 NIV). Biblical service means performing the works that "God prepared in advance for us to do," not "hustling" (Dr. Wheeler is also a former collegiate football coach) to find something to do so we can meet our daily service quota.

Born (Again) to Serve. King David acknowledged, "All the days ordained for me were written in your book before one of them came to be" (Ps. 139:16 NIV). When Mordecai urged Esther to plead with King Xerxes for mercy on the Jewish people, Mordecai said, "And who knows

---

9. Ibid., 58.

10. Swindoll, C. R., *Improving Your Serve: The Art of Unselfish Living* (Waco, Texas: Word, Inc. 1981), 98.

11. Ibid.

12. Beckett, J. D., *Loving Monday*. (Downers Grove, Illinois: InterVarsity Press 1998), 120.

but that you have come to royal position for such a time as this?" (Est. 4:14 NIV). The ultimate servant, Jesus, said of Himself, "For even the Son of Man did not come to be served, but to serve, and to give His life as a ransom for many" (Mark 10:45 NIV). If God's desire is for those who have been born again (John 3:3 NIV) to imitate His Son, then all believers are to be servants. Simon Peter's mother-in-law was quite literally saved to serve. In Luke we read that she was "suffering from a high fever" (Luke 4:38–39 NIV). Jesus healed her and "she got up at once and began to wait" on Him and everyone who had gathered in Simon Peter's home. The Apostle Paul declares in Galatians that God, "set [him] apart from birth and called [him] by grace" (Gal. 1:15 NIV) to serve the Gentiles by preaching the Gospel to them.

Prepared to Serve. The forty days Jesus spent in the desert being tempted by Satan were a means of preparation for both His ministry and crucifixion. The Gospels tell us that "Jesus often withdrew to lonely places and prayed" (Luke 5:16; Mark 1:35 NIV). After his Damascus road experience, Paul spent three years in Arabia preparing for his ministry to the Gentiles (Gal. 1:17–18 NIV). Prayer and meditation in the Word are two ways to prepare for service.

Humbled to Serve. The subtitle of Swindoll's book *Improving Your Serve* is *The Art of Unselfish Living*. Can you think of anyone you know who is both proud and unselfish? The two traits are incompatible. Jesus told his followers, "If anyone would come after me, he must deny himself and take up his cross daily and follow me" (Luke 9:23 NIV). Paul instructs us in Romans, "Do not think of yourself more highly than you ought… Honor one another above yourselves… Do not be proud" (Rom. 12:3, 9, 16 NIV). The Gospels provide examples of Peter exhibiting the very human trait of pride (e.g., "Even if all fall away on account of you, I never will" Matt. 26:33 NIV). Jesus knew that Peter needed to be humbled in order to become a bold servant following the Resurrection, thus He told Peter, "[B]efore the rooster crows, you will disown me three times" (Matt. 26:34 NIV). Jesus did not leave Peter in his dejected state, however. Jesus restored Peter to fellowship as recorded in John 21:15–17. These events exemplify the statement Jesus made to His host, a prominent Pharisee, "Everyone who exalts himself will be humbled, and he who humbles himself will be exalted" (Luke 14:11 NIV).

What Are the Consequences and Rewards of Servanthood? Swindoll lists four potential consequences of servanthood identified by the Apostle Paul in 2 Corinthians 4:8–9: affliction, confusion, persecution and rejection.[13] How are we to respond in these circumstances? According to James, we are to "consider it pure joy" (James 1:2 NIV). Once again, being a servant means behavior that is atypical by the world's standards. Is such a response possible for humans? When the Sanhedrin ordered Peter and the other apostles to be flogged for preaching the Gospel, they "rejoic[ed] because they had been counted worthy of suffering disgrace for the Name" (Acts 5:41 NIV).

Many companies offer rewards to loyal customers for their patronage. Airlines offer frequent-flyer miles, credit card companies offer premiums, and some fast-food restaurants offer free food to customers who fill up their punch-cards. The rewards program for the servants of Jesus Christ, however, makes all others pale by comparison! The rewards that await His servants include all of the following:

- *A mansion*: "In my Father's house are many mansions: if it were not so, I would have told you. I go to prepare a place for you" (John 14:1–3 KJV).

- *A full life*: "I have come that they may have life, and have it to the full" (John 10:9–11 NIV).

- *Eternal life*: "I give them eternal life, and they shall never perish; no one can snatch them out of my hand" (John 10:27–29 NIV).

- *More than we give up*: "'I tell you the truth,' Jesus replied, 'no one who has left home or brothers or sisters or mother or father or children or fields for me and the gospel will fail to receive a hundred times as much in this present age (homes, brothers, sisters, mothers, children and fields—and with them, persecutions) and in the age to come, eternal life'" (Mark 10:28–30 NIV).

- *All of our needs met*: "And my God will meet all your needs according to his glorious riches in Christ Jesus" (Phil. 4:19 NIV).

- *A crown*: "Now there is in store for me the crown of righteousness, which the Lord, the righteous Judge, will award to me on that day—and not only to me, but also to all who have longed for his appearing" (2 Tim. 4:8 NIV).

- *An inheritance*: "Now if we are children, then we are heirs—heirs of God and co-heirs with Christ, if indeed we share in his sufferings in order that we may also share in his glory" (Rom. 8:17 NIV).

---

13. Swindoll, C. R., *Improving Your Serve: The Art of Unselfish Living*. (Waco, Texas: Word, Inc. 1981), 178.

Part I: A Matter of Character

And this list is not exhaustive! Paul, the self-described "servant of Christ Jesus" (Rom. 1:1 NIV) wrote, "I consider that our present sufferings are not worth comparing with the glory that will be revealed in us" (Rom. 8:18 NIV). Not too bad of a rewards program for a servant!

Ronda O. Credille is an Associate Professor of Business Administration at Southwest Baptist University. She holds a BS from Southwest Baptist University, an MBA from Drury College and the PhD from the University of Nebraska.

3

Respect

"Slaves, obey your human masters with fear and trembling, in the sincerity of your heart, as to Christ. 6 Don't [work only] while being watched, in order to please men, but as slaves of Christ, do God's will from your heart. Render service with a good attitude, as to the Lord and not to men."
—Eph. 6:5–7

"Therefore, to you who believe, He is precious; but to those who are disobedient."
—1 Pet. 2:17 NKJV

"You shall rise before the gray headed and honor the presence of an old man, and fear your God: I am the LORD."
—Lev. 19:32 NKJV

All I'm Asking For

Susan Debauche

Respect. Such a simple word. Unfortunately, the word is becoming somewhat outdated in our society. Many just don't take it as seriously as they should. Aretha Franklin asked for—actually demanded—respect. But it was all she really did insist upon. Comedian Rodney Dangerfield complained that it was the one thing he couldn't get. His whole act was built upon his tagline, "I don't get no respect." Both Franklin and Dangerfield longed for respect, but they are not alone. Yet, in many ways, it seems that our society has taken a step backward in regard to showing respect for others.

On a practical level, respect includes taking someone's feelings, needs, thoughts, ideas, wishes, and preferences into consideration. Giving someone respect demonstrates that we value the person as well as his thoughts and feelings. If we truly respect someone, we acknowledge him, listen to him, and are truthful with him. Respect also allows us to accept a person's individuality and idiosyncrasies.

I am convinced that every human deserves respect, from those in positions of authority to the least powerful among us—especially the least powerful. Respect is demonstrated through our behavior toward another person; respect is also felt by the recipient. Many of us act in ways that are considered respectful, yet we seem to have the ability also to feel respect for someone. We seem to perceive when we are respected by someone else.

As a college professor, I have had the privilege to teach students from all over the world. I especially enjoy having students from the South in my classes. Their southern customs and manners are refreshing; they answer with "Yes, ma'am," or "Yes, sir." They seem inclined toward respectful behavior, at least in the classroom. But this respect isn't limited to a region. I grew up as a Northerner—a Wisconsinite—and I was taught the practice of respect in responding to my elders, too. But for some reason the practice just seems to be in short supply now.

Respect is a boomerang. You must send it out before it comes back to you. Respect cannot be demanded or forced. Respecting those in authority may seem like common sense, but many never learned that lesson. I grew up with the philosophy that a person must earn your respect; it's not something that is freely given. This philosophy made sense to me and it seemed fairly easy to grasp. However, I should have known that if it was easy, it probably wasn't right. Not until I left home to attend college in another state did I begin to reconsider this philosophy.

At the Christian university I attended, an amazingly wise teacher used the Bible to teach us some principles in economics. One of the principles he taught us was that it is biblical to pay taxes. That was an interesting concept to me, but I was struck by the scriptural mandate to do so and impressed with the relationship this had to respect. My professor used the scriptures found in Matthew in which Jesus says, "Give to Caesar what is Caesar's, and to God what is God's" (Matt. 22:15–22). He showed us how people who are put in a position of authority over us were put in that position by God, and that we are to respect the position God has put them in.

The truth of this really hit home and extends beyond his example. God put our parents, teachers, bosses, and government officials in the position they are in, and we are to respect them for that reason alone. Despite our affinity for someone in authority over us, we are commanded to respect them. By respecting those authorities, we are in turn respecting God, who has sovereignly placed them in their positions. Conversely, disrespecting authorities—no matter how much we dislike or disagree with them demonstrates disrespect for God.

The Bible makes several references to respect. "Each of you must respect his mother and father" (Lev. 19:3). "Rise in the presence of the aged, show respect for the elderly and revere your God" (Lev. 19:32). This notion of freely giving respect is contrary to our human nature; but it is clearly what the Bible calls us to do. Ephesians states, "Slaves obey your earthly masters with respect and fear, and with sincerity of heart just as you would obey Christ. Obey them not only to win their favor when their eyes are on you, but like slaves of Christ, doing the will of God from your heart. Serve wholeheartedly, as if you were serving the Lord, not men" (Eph. 6:5–7). Peter wrote, "Slaves, submit yourselves to your masters with all respect, not only to those who are good, but also to those who are harsh" (1 Pet. 2:17). In our own society, it might be helpful to read this as, "Employees, submit yourselves to your bosses with all respect. . . ." Talk about a tough command!

Inevitably, someone will object at this point and ask, "What about the times when someone in authority asks us to do something that is contrary to what God has commanded?" In these situations, we are expected to obey God and to follow His commands, even if it means going against a person in authority over us. Even then, however, God expects us to do this in a respectful manner. Too often though, this question is just a diversion from the command to show respect to those in authority. Too often, this objection is raised in an attempt to justify a person's own inability or unwillingness to respect those in authority over them.

Our nature is selfish. We want to be first. Most people, especially in our Western culture, have a fierce independence; we want to control our own lives, our own destinies, and our own conduct. We tend to resist those who are placed above us. Yet, the Word clearly commands us to respect others. Is it tough? Many times it is. Perhaps as professionals we should keep this in mind as we govern, supervise, and direct those who have been assigned to our own areas.

As a Christian professional, do you demonstrate respect to those in authority over you? What about to those who report to you? Are you the kind of supervisor that has earned the respect of your subordinates? Has the "boomerang" of respect not come back to you because you've never sent it? If you consider yourself a servant of Christ, the practice of respect should become more and more natural as you mature in your spiritual walk with God. Respect should become one of the most natural things a Christian exercises. Respect should become a natural habit. The world is full of hurting people. Women cry out that all they want is a little respect. Men complain that they never get any respect. Respect others. In so doing, you respect the Lord.

Susan Debauche is Chair and Professor of Business Administration at Southwest Baptist University. She holds a BA from Southwest Baptist University, the MSE from Central Missouri State University and the EdD from the University of Arkansas.

4

Charity

"In every way I've shown you that by laboring like this,
it is necessary to help the weak and to keep in mind
the words of the Lord Jesus, for He said,
'It is more blessed to give than to receive.'"
—Acts 20:35

"The wicked borrow and do not repay,
but the righteous give generously."
—Ps. 37:21 NIV

"A generous man will prosper;
he who refreshes others will himself be refreshed."
—Prov. 11:25 NIV

"When you reap the harvest of your land,
do not reap to the very edges of your field
or gather the gleanings of your harvest.
Do not go over your vineyard a second time
or pick up the grapes that have fallen.
Leave them for the poor and the alien.
I am the LORD your God."
—Lev. 19:9–10 NASB

"No one is useless in this world
who lightens the burden of it to anyone else."
—Charles Dickens

Charity:
Preserving the Dignity of Work

David Wesley Whitlock

Years ago, I heard a preacher tell about one of his children who had a habit of giving away everything he had. Whenever children would come to visit, his son would empty his piggybank and load his friends down with his savings. The preacher made the statement that of all his children, he prayed God would make that child rich. He explained that he prayed that prayer because that child knew how to give it away. What a refreshing attitude. I suspect that child had a deeper understanding of wealth and blessings than most adults. He seemed to understand that even if he had given away everything he had, the truth was that his daddy had more. The child was focused on how much he had. And when you're focused on what you have, instead of what you don't, you are free to give and free to share.

Most people are consumed with the opposite attitude. Get. Grab. Hoard. Keep. Our sin nature is selfish. Our old nature is stingy. Our natural inclination is to try to get more and more and more. Some going into the workforce for the first time will have the tendency to adopt that same mindset. Others going to college with the idea of getting a career instead of an education will be tempted to major in consumption, and to adopt careers that provide the opportunity to grab, hoard, and keep.

The irony is that the more we get, the more we think we need. We see this tendency even in the beginning with the story of Adam and Eve. God gave Adam and Eve everything they could ever need. The whole world was theirs to enjoy. They were rich and living in paradise. But when Satan approached them, he convinced them that they should want more. Don't you want more? Don't you want to be like God, to know good and evil? They gave in to the seduction of more. But as Adam and Eve discovered, the seduction of wanting more and more, and better and bigger is a trap. My hope is that we can readjust our thinking. The world has its standards. God's standards are different.

Part I: A Matter of Character

Jesus taught that the last shall be first. He taught that if you want to be the greatest, you must become the least, you must be a servant. In the Old Testament we read, "There is one who scatters yet increases more; and there is one who withholds more than is right, but it leads to poverty. The generous soul will be made rich, and he who waters will also be watered himself" (Prov. 11:24–25). What a contrast. The one who is generous, who gives away, will be given even more, but the one who is stingy and selfish will suffer poverty. God's ways are different than the world's ways, and God's people are different than the world. Therefore, the ways of God's people ought to stand in stark contrast to the world.

One way in which the people of God are to be different from the world in which they live has to do with work and the rewards and blessing received from our work. Our attitude about work and the blessings we receive from work are to be governed by God's laws. One illustration of this is found in Leviticus. Of all the books of the Bible, most people describe Leviticus as the most difficult to understand. It is probably fair to say that many have heard no sermons or at most, a handful of teachings expositing the book of Leviticus. It is filled with strange laws and commands governing the actions of the people of God during Old Testament times. It seems archaic and to have little relevance to our lives in these days. Many wonder what it's all about and whether it even relates to a Christian in the modern world.

The book of Leviticus is a book about worshipping a holy God, and we can learn much from our ancestors in the faith. Its precepts were originally for the Hebrew people just after their exodus from Egypt. They were camping at the base of Mount Sinai, and for many years, they were taught and molded into a nation that belonged to God, a unique nation that would be governed by God's standards, God's ways. They would be separated, different from the world around them. They would be governed by Ten Commandments. They would obey specific commands related to health, relationships, worship, and work.

Leviticus describes the ministry of the Levites, the tribe that was responsible for carrying out the functions of the priesthood and sacrificial offerings for sin. Among the laws about offerings, sacrifices, dietary laws, childbirth, diseases and health, crime and punishment, feasts, religious ceremonies, there are commands on relationships with one another, and on our moral and ethical behavior. One such principle governing the duty to provide and care for those less fortunate is taught in Leviticus. "When you reap the harvest of your land, you are not to reap to the very edge of your field or gather the gleanings of your harvest. You must not strip your vineyard bare or gather its fallen grapes. Leave them for the poor and the foreign resident; I am the LORD your God" (Lev. 19:9–10).

In this passage about sowing and reaping, we are introduced to the peculiar practice of allowing the poor, the widowed, and the stranger to gather grain in one's fields. We know this custom from the story of Ruth, who as a foreigner and a widow in Bethlehem, Judah, went into the fields to pick the missed grain from the reapers. Among the principles taught in this Levitical requirement are truths that relate to our lives as people called by Christ to be unique and different from the world around us.

First, this passage illustrates that work is a sacred responsibility. Work is good, right, and honorable. Work is required. Levitical law demanded that the owner of a field plant the whole field, but when harvest time came, the corners were to be left unharvested. They were for the poor and needy to harvest. It was a safety net for those without. Even the missed and dropped grain was to be left for the poor as well. It was a fair and equitable welfare system. But there was no command that the field's owner was required to harvest the corners of the field and then hand over the grain and the fruit to the needy. No command was given that the missed and dropped grain should be gleaned and then handed over to the poor. That would have robbed the poor of the opportunity and the dignity to work.

Many operate under the notion that society owes them something. Our own nation has, in an attempt to provide for those who are needy and poor, an entire class of dependents who have been enslaved by a perverted welfare system. I am convinced that God's word teaches that nothing is owed to us apart from work; that apart from the infirmed and disabled, people are required to work for what they receive. While some are prevented from contributing and from working because of strange laws and unreasonable requirements, far too many have chosen or been forced not to work. This kind of attitude and decision is not to be found among the people of God. The unharvested corners of the field, and the dropped and missed grain left in the field, are a testament to the notion that one is required to work, to earn his or her own way.

However, though the totality of the Bible teaches that God does not value slothfulness and laziness, it also teaches the imperative and responsibility to give out of God's blessings. Many readily affirm the notion of work as good, honorable, and a sacred obligation. Many embrace the notion that if one does not work, one does not eat. But this passage also clearly teaches that, as God's people, we are responsible to provide for those less fortunate. The corners of our fields are to be used for the benefit of others. The corners of the fields belonging to God's people should be used to provide for the welfare of the needy and the poor.

As soon as we get irritated with the state of government welfare programs, we need to quickly turn our attention to the church. If the church had been providing for the poor all along, there would have been no need for government involvement. The quickest way to reverse poverty is for the church to step in and do what God has commanded us all along. The quickest way to solve a perverted welfare program is for God's people to provide the corners of their fields to those who are without in order that they might have the opportunity to work and earn their way. The unharvested corners and the grain left in the field are a testimony that God will not tolerate stinginess and selfishness; that we who are blessed are commanded to provide for the welfare of others. Our responsibility as a Christian is to give out of the blessings God has given us.

Leviticus points to the absolute sanctity, strictness, and holiness required to worship Jehovah God. It points out a standard that is impossible for us to achieve in our current nature as sinful creatures. But the good news is that Jesus achieved it for us. Jesus met the standard. Jesus fulfilled all of the laws and requirements, including those found in Leviticus. We are under a new covenant through Jesus Christ, but the spirit of the law still holds relevance for our lives. The precepts recorded in the law are still to govern the lives of His people. Leviticus teaches us how we should relate to one another, treat one another, and provide for one another.

Among the lessons we can glean from Leviticus are these: Work is honorable and ordained of God. Work allows us to participate in the blessings and rewards of God. The blessings and rewards of God are meant to be shared. Living according to God's ways results in this wonderful promise from the one true God, Jehovah, the maker of heaven and earth: "I am the Lord your God." And in Jehovah's eyes, it is our responsibility to work. Nothing is owed to us apart from work. Nothing is free, save the most important thing in the world. The only thing in life that is free is the one thing which you could never earn by work—salvation and righteousness in the sight of God. While all of our works are as filthy rags, Christ grace gives us what we cannot earn.

Believers who have trusted Jesus and surrendered their lives to Him must remind themselves that it is their responsibility to give out of God's blessings—to use the corners of their fields for the benefit of others.

Besides, the truth is that Christians could give everything they have, and yet their Father in heaven still has more. God is the provider of our blessings, and believers simply cannot out-give or out-bless the Father.

David Wesley Whitlock serves as the Associate Provost, Dean of the College of Business and Computer Science, and Professor of Business Administration at Southwest Baptist University. He holds the BS and MBA from Southeastern Oklahoma State University, and the PhD from the University of Oklahoma.

5

Faithfulness

"Flee from youthful passions, and pursue righteousness, faith, love, and peace, along with those who call on the Lord from a pure heart."
—2 Tim. 2:22

"If we do not worship God somewhere
we will soon not worship Him anywhere."
—Herschel H. Hobbs

"Like anybody I would like to live a long life—longevity has its place. But I'm not concerned about that now. I just want to do God's will."
—Martin Luther King, Jr.,
speaking in Memphis, TN
the night before he was killed, April 4, 1968

"What is God's will for my life? Is not the best question to ask. I think the right question is simply, 'what is God's will?' Once I know God's will, then I can adjust my life to Him and His purposes."
—Henry Blackaby

"He is no fool who give what he cannot keep,
to gain what he cannot lose."
—Jim Elliott

"Man is born with his back toward God. When he truly repents, he turns around and faces God. Repentance is a change of mind . . . repentance is the tear in the eye of faith."
—Dwight L. Moody

A Picture of Faithfulness

Rodney Reeves

FAITHFULNESS IS one of those words we all use, but have a hard time defining. We think we know what we mean when we say, "He's a faithful guy," or "She's a faithful friend." But what we really mean is that he's reliable or she's loyal—but these qualities are not the same as faithfulness. Reliability could be a function of habit; loyalty often involves shared interests. Faithfulness derives from something more. The Pharisees were reliable. They fasted twice a week, prayed twice per day. The twelve were loyal to Jesus. They followed him wherever he went (except to the cross!). But, when we consider the gospel story, few would describe either group as faithful. This is why I think some of us are confused about what it means to be faithful to God.

Sadly, some may think of faithfulness as a bribe, a *quid pro quo* arrangement with God. "I will do what He wants of me so that He will do what I want of Him." In this case, faithfulness degenerates to a form of manipulation, where we try to bend God to our will, placating Him with acts of obeisance. We count on an all-seeing, all-knowing God to repay us for services rendered. Obedience is necessity. Compliance is strategy. Like spoiled children, we think we've figured out the game of reward. Like opportunistic employees, we know how to work the system. In this unholy role reversal, God becomes our debtor. We make demands. So, we open our hands as we bend our knee.

Others prefer to speak of faithfulness as an investment strategy. Doing the right thing is a practical matter. Sin has its consequences. Wickedness leads to misery. Fools persist in such destructive behavior. Only the wise are prosperous. So, the faithful look for dividends in clean living as we point out the downside of a reckless life. We see how the vacuous pursuit of selfishness turns restless seekers into narcissistic consumers. We know immediate gratification never satisfies. So, in defiant obedience we sneer at the shortsighted foolishness of those who waste their lives on wanton pleasures. "Yeah, they may look like they're having fun; but, deep down, they must be miserable." Trying to convince ourselves, we repeat the mantra: faithfulness requires patience. We count on the fact that evil catches up with rebels. What goes around comes around. Righteousness will bring its own rewards. Eventually, everyone will get what they deserve.

But, what happens when the wicked die at a ripe old age, enjoying their worldly vices till the end? What do we say when faithfulness to God *doesn't* pay, when God doesn't keep his end of our bargain? Why do bad things happen to good people? Indeed, after considering the injustices that accompany our so-called "faithfulness," some may resonate with the Preacher who said, "I have seen everything during my lifetime of futility; there is a righteous man who perishes in his righteousness, and there is a wicked man who prolongs his life in his wickedness. Do not be excessively righteous, and do not be overly wise. Why should you ruin yourself?" (Eccl. 7:15–16 NASB).

If doing the right thing makes a difference, why doesn't God reward the faithful for making a difference? Shouldn't a faithful life curry the favor of God? We know God loves all people, but shouldn't He love us more? Some may be tempted to join the chorus of the priests who said, "It is vain to serve God. What do we profit by keeping his command or by going about as mourners before the Lord of hosts? Now we count the arrogant happy; evildoers not only prosper, but when they put God to test they escape" (Mal. 3:14–15 NRSV).

This is why I like the way the Psalmist describes the faithful as those who "stand by their oath even to their hurt" (Ps. 15:4 NRSV). Faithfulness is not a matter of doing the right thing so that we may gain an advantage with God. In fact, when I consider the faithful (especially the heroes of the Bible), it has become ever more apparent to me that the obedient rarely got what they deserved. The prophets were murdered. Jesus was crucified. Paul was imprisoned. John was exiled. Where's the justice, the payoff, the reward? Why did God let this happen, over and over again? Suffering and death are not very appetizing carrots to dangle in front of sons and daughters of heaven. Who would be faithful for that? Only those who know what faithfulness is: to be faithful is to be full of faith.

Faithful sons and daughters are full of faith. They trust completely. They believe thoroughly. They have faith no matter what. And, what do they believe? Not only do they believe that God turns evil into good (Gen. 50:20; Rom. 8:28), and that history has a divine purpose (Jer. 29:11; Eph. 1:9–11). The faithful believe the gospel of Jesus is the story that must be played out in the lives of every follower of Christ. The death, burial, and resurrection of Christ is the predestined life of those who belong to Christ. The cross was no accident. Easter is no "plan B." God wasn't working "on the fly" when He built the temple we call "salvation." In fact, the gospel is what God had planned all along—not only how He would save us when we died, but also how He saves us as we live. Paul called it being "crucified with Christ" (Gal. 2:2). For him, the gospel was a *pattern* to follow (Phil. 3:17), a life to be imitated (1 Cor. 11:1)—to see things like he saw them: "have this mindset among yourselves which was also in Christ Jesus" (Phil. 2:5[1]). How did Jesus and Paul see life the same way?

Paul believed what happened to Jesus would also happen to him, to Timothy, to Epaphroditus, to all of his converts. It's a story of humiliation leading to exaltation, death producing life, shame morphing into honor, loss reckoned as gain, weakness becoming strength. This is not giving to get. This is giving up. Paul realized "the world has been crucified to me, and I to the world" (Gal. 6:14 NASB). This is why, when Paul experienced "bad things," he believed he was receiving the grace of God (2 Cor. 11:24–12:10). Imprisonment did not impede the gospel—who can chain the good news of Christ (Phil. 1:12–18)? Waiting for his Roman trial, Paul saw his imprisonment as a confirmation of the gospel. His chains proved he was imitating Christ; what happened to Paul is what happened to Jesus (Phil. 2:7–8; 3:8–10). Live the gospel and Jewish leaders will beat you, Roman rulers will kill you. The veil of the temple was ripped in half; every knee will bow to Christ (not Caesar!). This is the way it's supposed to be—it is predestined. It's what Paul believed. And, because he was full of this faith, he endured all things, longing to know the "power of His resurrection and the fellowship of His sufferings, being conformed to His death" (Phil. 3:10 NASB). Paul believed bearing the cross of Christ would mean his resurrection. Totally.

Can you imagine how frustrating it must have been for Paul's opponents? Like Job's counselors, they must have interpreted the horrible things that happened to Paul as God's just punishment. The way they saw it, God couldn't get it through Paul's thick skull that He wasn't pleased with the rebel apostle who shared table with Gentiles, ate pork, and worshipped God on the wrong day (Sunday!). Beaten and humiliated, shipwrecked (who controls the wind and the sea?) and imprisoned, nothing could stop him. Paul fully believed he was on a mission for Christ: not only to tell the good news, but to *be* the good news. This is why, whenever a cross was placed on the back of the apostle, he embraced it with the passionate kiss of his life. For him, a crucified life was the only way to live.

So, this is faithfulness. Believing God no matter the circumstances. Doing the right thing simply because it's right. Knowing bad things will

---

1. Author's translation.

happen to good people. Denying the ways of the world. Seeing the gospel as a way of life. Reckoning loss as gain, humility as honorable, sacrifice as blessing, weakness as strength. Indeed, if the world has been crucified to us, and we to the world, then everything is upside down. Even though the world says, "Get ahead by promoting yourself," we will promote others because the things of this world don't matter. Even though the world says, "Get what you can while you can," we will be spent for Christ because He was spent for us. Even though the world says, "create your own destiny," we will be conformed to the image of God's Son. For, when it's all said and done, Jesus is what faithfulness looks like.

Rodney Reeves serves as the Dean of The Courts Redford College of Theology and Ministry, and as Professor of Biblical Studies at Southwest Baptist University. He holds a BA from Southwest Baptist University, the MDiv and PhD from Southwestern Baptist Theological Seminary, and has completed additional study at Oxford University.

6

Truthfulness

"You will know the truth,
and the truth will set you free."
—John 8:32

"Truthful lips will be established forever,
but a lying tongue is only for a moment."
—Prov. 12:19 NASB

"[G]uide me in your truth and teach me,
for you are God my Savior,
and my hope is in you all day long."
—Ps. 25:5 NIV

"Honesty is the first chapter in the book of wisdom."
—Thomas Jefferson

The Truth Shall Set You Free

Bart C. Craytor

The court demanded an answer. "How do you plead? Guilty or not guilty?" With a lump in her throat she dropped her head and tears filled her eyes. She began to tremble as her fate hung in the balance, completely in the hands of the Judge. With quivering lips she confessed, "Guilty your honor."

"Are you pleading guilty because you are guilty and for no other reason?" the Judge asked.

She whispered a simple and nearly silent, "Yes." Her eyes could no longer hold the tears and they began to stream down her face to the podium as she steadied her stance. She felt nauseous, faint, vulnerable, and weak.

Because a co-defendant was denying his own crime, the prosecutor requested to question her on the record. The prosecutor could then utilize her statements to stop the co-defendant from continuing his lies and denials. She was directed to the witness chair, sworn to tell the truth and then sat nervously awaiting the inquisition.

I recently had the privilege of representing this very defendant. She was a nurse who served in a Texas penal institution. During her work she became acquainted with the prisoners and was charmed by one in particular—the co-defendant. The prisoner's friendly banter, pledge of unending love and his compliments on her attractiveness delighted the woman and increased her self esteem. The convicted felon encouraged the relationship with proclamations of love and romance. After several months of visits and nearly daily exchanges of notes, glances, and casual touches, she was thoroughly smitten. He then convinced her to bring him a cellular telephone so they could talk on nights and weekends. She secured a cellular telephone and smuggled it to him, knowing that this was against the law and endangering her co-workers. Such devices can be used to coordinate escapes, riots, abductions, assaults against guards and other prisoners within the confines of the gray walls. They are also used to facilitate delivery of illicit substances to the prisoners. Her emotions incited her to violate the law and put her at risk of a felony conviction.

Part I: A Matter of Character

It wasn't long before the cell phone was discovered and after a short investigation the nurse was implicated, then indicted for delivery of a forbidden item in a penal institution. The factual issues were compelling and a conviction would be certain if the case was tried. As her attorney, I advised her that she would best be served to enter a plea and seek probationary options to avoid a felony conviction. The prosecutor demanded that she serve four months in prison in addition to fines, fees, and being placed on probation for ten years. Her only hope to avoid a felony conviction was to accept the plea offer and pray that the court defer adjudication of guilt until the probationary period was over, leaving her without a judgment of guilt if she successfully completed her probation.

She confided that if she were to be imprisoned for two weeks, much less four months she would lose her home to foreclosure, her car would be repossessed, and she would lose her job and possibly never again work as a nurse. Her nursing skills were never questioned; it was her character and reputation at issue. She was at risk of losing her liberty, possessions, and dignity. She faced the possibility of being a convicted felon. She never had any prior contact with law enforcement. Not even a parking ticket. Her past record was spotless. She was a person of character who simply made a mistake—a mistake that could potentially cost her everything. To avoid a conviction, her only realistic hope was to face the judge in a plea and pray for deferred adjudication.

The day for entering the plea arrived with dreaded anticipation. She mentally prepared for the possibility of incarceration. After several questions regarding how the cell phone was procured and delivered, the prosecutor asked if she was aware that a telephone was a forbidden item to possess in a penal institution. She responded affirmatively. He then asked if she was advised of this before she committed this crime. Again she truthfully responded, "Yes, they told me when I started there."

The prosecutor then asked questions that served to reveal the felon's deceptive courtship, praises, and false promises. How her heart had wanted to believe that she had found true love. How she fell for the lies and ruses. She affirmed each question she was asked. The prosecutor then turned to the Judge and with emphatic declaration exclaimed that the honesty of this woman had convinced him to abandon the request for a jail sanction and that the State would not oppose the deferral of adjudication pending successful completion of the probation. I added her spotless past as an indication that she did not have the demeanor for any continued criminal enterprise. She made an error in judgment, albeit a serious error. But it was not one that should suffer the label of a felon. Deferral of a conviction was

Truthfulness

warranted and worthy, and the purpose of justice would not be served by her incarceration.

The court accepted her plea of guilty and ordered her to ten years of probation because of the severity of the offense being committed by a professional. A professional is judged according to a higher standard. She was educated and knowingly and intentionally committed a crime against the peace and dignity of the state. After ordering her to pay fines and court costs, he then announced that he was not going to issue judgment of conviction but would defer judgment while she successfully completed probation. Upon successful completion of the probation, the indictment would be dismissed and she would not be a convicted felon. Because the State forwent its request for a prison sanction, no jail time was ordered. We both breathed a sigh of relief.

We had just witnessed an example of the truth setting one free. Had the prosecutor not been convinced by her unwavering honesty—even when it was adverse to her interest to make such admissions—she likely would have been imprisoned for at least four months and quite possibly lost everything. "And you shall know the truth and the truth shall make you free" (John 8:32). Her truthfulness convinced the court to take mercy on her.

What is truthfulness? It is generally accepted as an individual character trait manifesting in constant and consistent promotion of fact and disregarding or avoiding what is false. Honesty, righteousness and holy are other words associated with truthfulness. In John 8:32, Jesus was referring to the truthfulness of the gospel. Here the concept of truthfulness encompasses the belief in Christ's atonement of our sins, redemption to God the Father of our eternal lives, and our calling to live as Christ lived. It includes the gift of the Holy Spirit Who God sent to live in each believer. Jesus promised to " [P]ray [to] the Father, and He will give you another Helper, that He may abide with you forever—the Spirit of truth, whom the world cannot receive, because it neither sees Him nor knows Him; but you know Him, for He dwells with you and will be in you" (John 14:16–17 NKJV).

Two people may witness an incident and each offer details that seem to be mutually exclusive to the other's description. Each may believe his or her own description is the absolute truth and the other's view is false or mistaken. Courts recognize that our ability to perceive, remember and communicate perceptions can lead to totally different conclusions as to a particular incident. The real world limits our examination to what our senses allow. We see what people do and say. Physical limitations, biases and prejudices complicate our observations by obscuring, tainting and interfering with the truth.

Part I: A Matter of Character

So what is a Christian to do? First, we must recognize that the truths in the Bible do not vary over time. The truths in the Bible are absolute. Study the Word, receive its mandates, and discover the truth between its covers[1]. Adopt the character traits of honesty and righteousness. Practice truthfulness. My nurse-client demonstrates the dichotomy between a lie that beguiled her and the truth that saved her. She fell victim to the lies of a deceiver, but the truth saved her from ruin. Her story illustrates the difference between a life free from former fault contrasted with an unrepentant prisoner. She had been susceptible to a con. But her resolute stance to abide in honesty, even when it appeared against her own self-interest, won over the prosecutor. Anchor your soul to the solid rock, fear not the waves of tribulation, for tribulation is only for a season, the truth will stand forever.

Bart C. Craytor is an attorney with Dunbar, Craytor and Morgan in Texarkana, Texas. He holds BS and MAS from Southeastern Oklahoma State University, and the JD from Oklahoma City University School of Law.

---

1. "All Scripture is given by inspiration of God, and is profitable for doctrine, for reproof, for correction, for instruction in righteousness" (2 Tim. 3:16 NKJV).

7

Humility

"And all of you clothe yourselves with humility toward one another, because God resists the proud, but gives grace to the humble."
—1 Pet. 5:5b

"We serve God whether people honor us or despise us, whether they slander us or praise us."
—2 Cor. 6:8 NLT

"I make it a point to cook and wait on tables, to spend time 'in the back of the house' with the folks who do the work every day. I've learned so much."
—Julia Steward,
CEO of IHOP

"Spiritual excellence is not about ascending the ladder of leadership to greatness. It is about descending the ladder of humility to servanthood."
—Patrick Morley

"God may have to weaken us and bring us down at the points where we thought we were strong in order that we may become truly strong in real dependence on himself."
—J. I. Packer,
in Never Beyond Hope

Humility

Attitude and Action

Rodger W. Minatra

"Do nothing out of rivalry or conceit, but in humility consider others as more important than yourselves. Everyone should look out not only for his own interests, but also for the interests of others" (Phil. 2:3-4). In the eulogy for President Reagan, the elder President Bush told the story of how not long after Reagan's surgery, which repaired the wounds he received in the assassination attempt on his life, his aides entered his hospital room and found him on his hands and knees. Worried that his nurse would get in trouble, President Reagan was cleaning up a water spill from the floor—an act of humility and character by a person of considered position and power. Such an action seems counter to our present culture. More times than not, our culture tells us that meekness is weakness, compassion is compromise, and submission is suicide. Humility is certainly not one of the praised character traits on Donald Trump's hit program, *The Apprentice*.

In a day and age when the use of the word *competition* is only outdone by the word *globalization*, it seems difficult to find a place for the word *humility*, especially in the world of business. Humility, defined as the condition of being humble, is often associated with meekness, submission, lowly rank or position, and self abasement. If this is humility, how can a Christian succeed in a world that seems to reward pride and aggressiveness?

The Bible tells us that humility is necessary for success. King Solomon, considered one of the richest and wisest men to ever live, addresses humility several times in the book of Proverbs. "The fear of the LORD is Wisdom's instruction, and humility comes before honor" (Prov. 15:33). "Before his downfall, a man's heart is proud, but before honor comes humility" (Prov. 18:12). "The result of humility is fear of the LORD, along with wealth, honor, and life" (Prov. 22:4). "Better to be lowly of spirit with the humble, than to divide plunder with the proud" (Prov. 16:19). "A person's pride will humble him, but a humble spirit will gain honor" (Prov. 29:23).

In each of these verses, humility precedes honor; and in one, it precedes wealth and life. All of these are included measurements in the sense of worldly success. The Bible also tells us that humility is part of the character of Christ Jesus. As Christians we measure our success by our Christlike character. Jesus himself encourages us to follow His example and take on the character of gentleness and humility. "Come to Me, all of you who are weary and burdened, and I will give you rest. All of you, take up My yoke and learn from Me, because I am gentle and humble in heart, and you will find rest for yourselves, For My yoke is easy and My burden is light" (Matt. 11:28–30).

In Christian circles, humility is often defined as avoiding false pride about our abilities or accomplishments. However, a deeper knowledge of the Christian faith informs that humility is more than refraining from bragging or boasting about our accomplishments. Scripture tells us to think of others as better than ourselves. I have often struggled with this verse, but have come to believe that humility is the realization that I cannot live in a sinful world and expect to accomplish anything good apart from God. William Wilberforce, credited with the abolition of slavery in Europe, wrote in his book *Real Christianity* (published in 1797), that our inability is our great asset; it creates a humility that becomes dependent on God's grace working in us. Likewise, in the first book of Corinthians, the Apostle Paul tells us that knowledge without humility leads to intellectual vanity.

Scripture also tells us that humility is both an attitude and action of obedience. "Make your own attitude that of Christ Jesus, who, existing in the form of God, did not consider equality with God as something to be used for His own advantage. Instead He emptied Himself by assuming the form of a slave, taking on the likeness of men. And when He had come as a man in His external form, He humbled Himself by becoming obedient to the point of death—even the death on a cross." (Phil. 2:5–8).

When I think of humility as an attitude and not just an action, it brings to mind a statement I read several years ago. Ethel Barrett, known as *The Story Lady*, was one of the most popular Christian personalities in America during the mid-twentieth century. She said, "Humility has its own form of pride." Growing up in a Christian family I was taught the importance of humility, and I've practiced it. Unfortunately, an anxious heart and a prideful desire can rob the most humble actions of their honor. "Humble your selves therefore under the mighty hand of God, so that He may exalt you in due time, casting all your care upon Him, because He cared about you." (I Pet. 5:6–7).

Humility is tough. It goes against the grain. We naturally tend toward being served rather than serving others. But a Christian ought to follow the example of our Lord who humbled Himself. Christian professionals should be the kind of people who never think so highly of themselves that they are unwilling to put others' needs ahead of their own or are unwilling to serve others. Christian professionals should be the type of people, who no matter what elevated station in life they may enjoy, might be found on their hands and knees mopping up a spill to spare someone else trouble.

Rodger W. Minatra is an Associate Professor of Business Administration at Southwest Baptist University. He holds a BS from Arizona State University, an MA from the University of Denver and the EdD from the University of North Texas.

8

Perserverance

"I press on toward the goal for the prize
of the upward call of God in Christ Jesus."
—Phil. 3:14 ESV

"Be persistent, whether the time is favorable or not."
—2 Tim. 4:2 NRSV

"Blessed is the man who perseveres under trial,
because when he has stood the test,
he will receive the crown of life
that God has promised to those who love him."
—James 1:12 NIV

"Suffering produces perseverance; perseverance, character,
and character, hope. And hope does not disappoint us,
because God has poured out His love into our hearts."
—Rom. 5:3–5 NIV

"Some men give up their designs when they have almost reached the
goal; while others, on the contrary obtain a victory by exerting,
at the last moment, more vigorous efforts than ever before."
—Herodotus

"If there is no struggle, there is no progress."
—Frederick Douglass

"Great hearts can only be made through great troubles."
—C. H. Spurgeon

"You can see God using some lives,
but into your life an obstacle has come
and you do not seem to be of any use.
Keep paying attention to the Source,
and God will either take you
round the obstacle or remove it."
—Oswald Chambers

"I do the very best I know how—the very best I can;
and I mean to keep doing so until the end.
If the end brings me out all right,
what's said against me won't amount to anything.
If the end brings me out wrong, ten angels swearing
I was right would make no difference."
—Abraham Lincoln

What Keeps You Going?

R. Stanton Norman

ONLY TWO men failed to return from the storied Lewis and Clark expedition of the early 1800s.[1] One man failed to return because he got sick and died. The other man failed to return because he was smitten. He had just seen the breadth and length of what would one day become the United States of America—from the Great Plains to the Rockies to the Columbia basin of Oregon to the Pacific Ocean. The vast wonders of the continent had a grip on his soul. So when Lewis and Clark set out for home, John Colter waved them good-bye. He stayed behind to explore the wide lands that were outside the scope of the expedition. He wanted to follow some of those trails and paddle up some of those rivers he had passed by on the way to the Pacific. Their wild beauty haunted him.

Colter trapped beaver in the virgin streams of the high country. He was the first white man to witness the geysers of Yellowstone. The young man's love affair with uncharted lands kept him in constant danger. Close encounters with monster grizzlies, churning white-water rapids, and always dangerous Indians tested his courage, pluck, and reflexes. As years went by, he gained a legendary status among his fellow trappers and mountain men—men not easily impressed. But the accomplishment that sealed Colter's reputation as a living legend was not a battle with a grizzly, shooting rapids in a fragile canoe, or scaling an unknown mountain range.

John Colter was best known for a single foot race. The account of the race would be told and retold around campfires from the Columbia to the Missouri. John Colter ran like few men in history had ever run; he was running for his life. Colter had been trapping beaver in a particular stream with an old friend from the Lewis and Clark expedition, John Potts. As they were canoeing down a stretch of river not far from what is today Bozeman, Montana, they heard a rustling in the brush on both sides of the riverbank. In the next instant, the two men were surrounded by Blackfeet Indians with drawn bows.

---

1. The following account of John Colter is excerpted from the work, Steve Farrar, *Finishing Strong: Going the Distance for Your Family* (Sister, OR: Multnomah Pub., 2000).

Part I: A Matter of Character

There was no time for escape downstream. Colter did the only thing he could have done; he headed for the bank. As they were getting out of the canoe, a large Blackfeet brave ran forward and snatched the rifle out of the hands of John Potts. Colter, a man of great physical strength and courage, knew that any sign of fear would only ensure their torturous death at the hands of these Blackfeet Indians. The desperate trapper grabbed the rifle and wrestled it away from the Indian, throwing the man to the ground in the process. Colter tossed the weapon to Potts and turned to confront the startled warriors.

Potts had seen enough and jumped into the canoe to make a getaway. "No!" shouted Colter, knowing there was no escape in that direction. Arrows rained into the canoe, killing Potts. The river current swept the canoe and the body of Colter's friend downstream. Colter himself stood on the bank, unarmed, and alone. The Blackfeet swarmed around him, stripped him naked, and then tied him down as they tried to determine what to do with him.

Some warriors shouted, "Skin him alive!" Others cried, "Beat him to death!" Still other braves roared, "Burn him alive!" Then one of the Blackfeet offered a creative idea. The chief approached Colter and asked him if he could run like a deer. Colter indicated that he was not as fast as a deer, but slow like a turtle. This was a lie, for Colter was a remarkably fast runner. The chief, however, took the bait and quickly led everyone to a nearby sandy plain. He made a mark in the ground, and his warriors toed the line. He then took Colter and gave him a three hundred-yard head start. The buck-naked Colter took off like a shot. Except for moccasins and loin cloths, the pursuing Blackfeet were as naked as Colter. Each warrior also carried his favorite weapon—and yearned for the honor of killing the white trapper.

The plain stretched ahead of Colter for six miles, dotted only by sagebrush and prickly pear. Shimmering on the horizon, however, Colter could see a line of trees on what must have been a bend of the river. John Colter focused on those trees and began the run of this life. Colter's bare feet were soon cut to bloody ribbons by sharp stones and prickly pear, but in this race there was no stopping. One mile passed. Two miles sped by. At approximately three miles, Colter looked back over his shoulder, for he could no longer hear the yelling of his pursuers or the slap of their moccasins in the dust. Only a handful of pursuers were still in the hunt, and they were a good distance away. One solitary brave, however, had closed to within two hundred yards. Colter's body was so stressed from the exertion of the chase that blood trickled from his mouth and nose.

At four miles, Colter looked back again. With protective moccasins on his feet, the Blackfeet brave had gained a lot of ground and was less than fifty yards away. Colter knew his broad, naked back was in range of the warrior's sharp lance. So, without any warning, the hunted man suddenly whirled and stopped. Colter faced the onrushing Indian and threw his hands up in the air as if to surrender. The shocked brave immediately threw his lance and stumbled head over heels as the weapon left his hand. The lance fell short, and Colter rushed and snatched it from the place where it landed. He then took the weapon and plunged it into his pursuer before the exhausted warrior could regain his footing. Colter drove the lance into his pursuers body with such force that the man was penned to the ground to die by his own weapon.

Summoning every ounce of strength he had left, Colter ran the remaining mile or so to the river and the stand of timber. A sandbar was in the middle of the stream, and at the head of this small island was a large raft of driftwood that had come down with the spring floods. Colter swam out to the raft, dove beneath it, and came up where several of the entangled logs formed a roof above his head. Here he waited for the pursuing Blackfeet, up to his neck in the icy waters under this makeshift shelter.

Colter soon heard the approaching Blackfeet. They swarmed around the river, onto the sandbar, and even stood upon the logs that covered his head. The enraged Indians could not, however, find him. The day was young, and his pursuers were anxious to avenge the death of their fallen comrade. The Blackfeet warriors kept up the hunt until late afternoon before finally withdrawing. Under the cover of darkness, John Colter swam downstream until he found a tiny stretch of bank concealed by trees and brush. Naked, half-frozen, and nearly delirious from exposure and loss of blood, Colter pulled himself out of the stream and lay gasping on the bank. He had no rifle, no food, no fire, no horse, no shoes, and no clothing. He had been stripped of everything he had but his will to live. John Colter was half-dead and 150 miles from the trading post at Bighorn. Seven days later, he walked naked, bleeding, and hungry into the Bighorn compound. In that moment, a living legend was born. Stripped of everything and against the worst odds imaginable, John Colter outran and outsmarted the pursuing Blackfeet for 156 miles. In spite of his circumstances, John Colter managed to persevere when many would have quit.

I must admit that there are days when certain aspects of this story resonate with me. For example, like Colter, I find myself in a "race" (life often has prolonged moments comparable to a marathon) not of my own choosing. Like Colter, the circumstances of my life's race are often unpleasant, uncomfortable, and even painful. In the race of life, however, there is no stopping for personal pain or discomfort. And like Colter, there

Part I: A Matter of Character

are days when the circumstances of life seem to pursue and hound me, and on occasion these people, events, or circumstances of life threaten to overwhelm me and derail me in my journey. What keeps you going when you want to quit? What keeps you in the race of life, even when every aspect of life (people, events, circumstances, etc.) would justify stopping and quitting? What keeps you going when every fiber of your being seems to scream, "Stop! The pain is too great. The circumstances are unbearable." How do you persist, or persevere, through this journey called life?

Fortunately for us, the Bible contains the accounts of the great men and women, or heroes, of the Christian faith. We find in their lives examples of the power of God sustaining them in the midst of their "race of life." In these biblical accounts, God reveals to us how He empowered and equipped these people to continue and finish their race until completion, even when their circumstances seemed to justify quitting. Although we could profitably focus on many candidates, I want to examine the life of an Old Testament saint named Caleb. His life is a model of perseverance. Although the circumstances of his life seemed insurmountable, God sustained and enabled Caleb to persevere in his walk of faith. In fact, because Caleb faithfully persevered, we can conclude that the end of his life was better than the beginning. I am confident that the power of God that sustained Caleb will likewise equip us to continue when we would rather stop.

> The descendants of Judah approached Joshua at Gilgal, and Caleb son of Jephunneh the Kenizzite said to him, "You know what the Lord promised Moses the man of God at Kadesh-barnea about you and me. I was 40 years old when Moses the Lord's servant sent me from Kadesh-barnea to scout the land, and I brought back an honest report. My brothers who went with me caused the people's hearts to melt with fear, but I remained loyal to the Lord my God. On that day Moses promised me, "The land where you have set foot will be an inheritance for you and your descendants forever, because you have remained loyal to the Lord my God. As you see, the Lord has kept me alive 45 years as He promised, since the Lord spoke this word to Moses while Israel was journeying in the wilderness. Here I am today, 85 years old. I am still as strong today as I was the day Moses sent me out. My strength for battle and for daily tasks is now as it was then. Now give me this hill country the Lord promised me on that day, because you heard then that the Anakim are there, as well as large fortified cities. Perhaps the Lord will be with me and I will drive them out as the Lord promised." Then Joshua blessed Caleb son of Jephunneh and gave him Hebron as an inheritance. Therefore, Hebron has belonged to Caleb son of

Jephunneh the Kenizzite as an inheritance to this day, because he remained loyal to the Lord, the God of Israel. Hebron's name used to be Kiriath-arba; Arba was the greatest man among the Anakim. After this, the land had rest from war (Josh. 14:6–14).

In this passage, we see the power of God motivating and sustaining Caleb over the course of a long life. Caleb persevered faithfully in the calling and tasks that God placed upon his life. What kept Caleb going? Caleb's perseverance in his life's mission was due to the faithfulness of God and these verses contain four primary lessons worth our attention.

Perseverance Is Grounded Upon the Faithfulness of God to His Word and Promises.

The first lesson illustrated in this passage is that perseverance in faithful service to God rests upon the certainty, or truthfulness, of the word of God. The dialogue between Caleb and Joshua reveals Caleb's deep conviction regarding his belief in the trustworthiness of God. For example, in verse six, Caleb states, ""You know *what the Lord promised Moses the man of God at Kadesh-barnea about you and me.*" In verse ten, Caleb declares, "As you see, the Lord has kept me alive 45 years *as He promised, since the Lord spoke this word* to Moses while Israel was journeying in the wilderness." Again, Caleb confesses his absolute trust in the sure word of God in verse twelve when he says, "Now give me this hill country *the Lord promised me* on that day, because you heard then that the Anakim are there, as well as large fortified cities. Perhaps the Lord will be with me and I will drive them out *as the Lord promised.*" Caleb structured the entirety of his life upon the premise that God is trustworthy and speaks absolute truth.

Perseverance is thus directly tied to the faithfulness of God. If we believe that God cannot or will not be faithful to His promises, our certainty to persevere in life is destroyed. If we believe God cannot be trusted to speak a truthful word, we have no basis to determine truth from falsehood, right from wrong. The conviction of Caleb to claim his inheritance is grounded upon his belief that God speaks truth and therefore will keep His promise to him. As believers, we also can find stability and direction for our life of faith when we embrace the truth of and live in the conviction that God can be trusted to keep His word. When God declares that He will keep and sustain us (John 10:13; Rom. 8:31–39), He can be absolutely trusted to keep His promise. We can therefore draw strength from His promises and continue in our life of discipleship when the occasions and circumstances of our life threaten to derail our journey. Always remember that the God who is all powerful and all truthful will be faithful to keep His promises to us. This truth will always overcome any occasional circumstance or unpleasant situation that confronts us in life.

The Faithfulness of God to His Word and Promises Elevates Our Perspective in Life.

The second lesson illustrated by this passage involving Caleb is that perspective is a powerful, determining factor for life and is derived from a right conviction regarding the word of God. Perspective is also directly connected to our ability to persevere. The gracious gift of perseverance rests upon the action of the Holy Spirit working in the life of the believer to change how that individual views his or her life and mission. Evidence of a *persevering perspective* is seen in Caleb's temporal assessment of God faithfulness. In verses six through nine, Caleb recounted the mighty works of God in Israel's recent history. In verses ten and eleven, Caleb assessed his current condition in light of the present faithfulness to God. Caleb believed that the God who made the promise of inheritance forty-five years ago would empower him for the mission he aspired to have. Likewise, in verse twelve, Caleb believed that the God who proved faithful in the past and present would also prove faithful for his impending mission of conquest. Caleb's future confidence in the empowerment of God rested upon the past and present faithfulness of God. Caleb believed God would equip him to take his inheritance because he had learned to trust God in past and present conditions. In this sense, a "persevering perspective" transforms our ability to view our past, present, and future in light of the faithfulness of God.

A *persevering perspective* also changes the way we assess our current situation. When we consider Caleb, we might be prone to see a man who was beyond the ability to accomplish his mission to take his inheritance. He was, after all, an elderly man, even by the standards of his day. "As you see, the Lord has kept me alive 45 years as He promised, since the Lord spoke this word to Moses while Israel was journeying in the wilderness. Here I am today, 85 years old" (Josh. 14:10). He would have been considered well beyond his physical prime and therefore unable to engage and sustain a military campaign. Whereas his contemporaries saw an old man, Caleb believed himself still fit for service and mission. This conviction is stated in verse eleven: "I am still as strong today as I was the day Moses sent me out. My strength for battle and for daily tasks is now as it was then." Caleb believed that he was prepared and ready to accomplish his mission.

The faithfulness of God to His word and promises instills within us a perspective to persist. The persevering work of God changed the way Caleb viewed himself and his ability to fulfill the will of God for his life. He did not see himself as an aged man ready to rest in life. He viewed himself as a warrior ready to battle for his inheritance. The persevering work of God will change how we see ourselves and the circumstances of our life. A *persevering perspective* is one means by which God empowers us such that we believe and do overcome those difficulties and dilemmas. We assess problems differently. We view our calling in life differently. We interpret our ability to succeed in life differently. The gracious work of perseverance therefore transforms our perspective of ourselves, our world, and our mission in the world. Godly success will only come to those who look at life through the eyes of a persevering perspective.

The Faithfulness of God to His Word and Promises Sustains Us in Times of Great Waiting.

A third lesson found in the passage about Caleb is that the faithfulness of God to His word and promises not only instilled within Caleb a persevering perspective, God's faithfulness also sustained him through a time of significant waiting. Notice the chronology of events mentioned by Caleb. In verses five and six Caleb stated, "You [Joshua] know what the Lord promised Moses the man of God at Kadesh-barnea about you and me. I was 40 years old when Moses the Lord's servant sent me from Kadesh-barnea to scout the land, and I brought back an honest report." He then remarked in verse ten, "As you see, the Lord has kept me alive 45 years as He promised, since the Lord spoke this word to Moses while Israel was journeying in the wilderness. Here I am today, 85 years old." Caleb stated that the reason for his delayed entrance into the Promised Land was because "my brothers who went with me caused the people's hearts to melt with fear, but I remained loyal to the Lord my God." He further stated in nine, "On that day Moses promised me, 'The land where you have set foot will be an inheritance for you and your descendants forever, because you have remained loyal to the Lord my God.'" Caleb's reward would come, but it would be a delayed reward. Hem, therefore, was consigned to wait for an entire generation of unfaithful Hebrews to die in the wilderness before he could enter the land of promise. Caleb would wait forty years before his feet ever entered the land, and he would then wait an additional five years before receiving his inheritance.

The concept of a sustained wait is quite foreign to our culture. In our world of instant gratification, delayed reward seems at best, an unfair act, or at worst, an unjust punishment. A period of prolonged, sustained waiting is perceived as cruel. What kept Caleb going each day in the wilderness as he waited for the fulfillment of the judgment of God? What sustained him? What would sustain us in a period of great waiting? I again appeal to the faithfulness of God as that activity which works within us a perseverance that sustains us in times of great waiting. Sometimes the timing of God is immediate and instantaneous. The Bible contains numerous examples of the quick, direct intervention of God. The Bible also contains, however, numerous examples where the intervention of God in an event or the fulfillment of God to a promise requires a lifetime of waiting. These periods of sustained waiting seem to me to be more normative than the occasional immediate interventions of God. God graciously works in the life of a believer to bring about a perseverance that sustains us through those prolonged periods of trial and difficulty. When our lives are grounded upon the faithful God, we can endure times of great waiting. The reality of the faithfulness of God is greater than the reality of the trying, difficult times of life in which we often find ourselves.

The Faithfulness of God to His Word and Promises Empowers Us To Confront the Major Obstacles of Life.

The final truth regarding perseverance that we can glean from this passage is that the faithfulness of God to His word and promises empowers us to confront the major obstacles of life. One of the major barriers to the entrance of the Israelites into the Promised Land was their concern about "the giants of the land." In Numbers 13:32–33, ten of the twelve spies cried, "The land we passed through to explore is one that devours its inhabitants, and all the people we saw in it are men of great size. We even saw the Nephilim there. . . . To ourselves we seemed like grasshoppers, and we must have seemed the same to them." The presence of giants in the land caused great fear among the covenant community. In fact, the presence of these large warrior people appears to be a major reason why the majority of Israelites refused to enter the land. The resulting distrust in the faithfulness of God to His promise that He would give the land to the Israelites was the basis for the judgment of God against them. This pronouncement is found in Numbers: "Yes, as surely as I live . . . none of the men who have seen my glory and the signs I performed in Egypt will ever see the land I swore to give their fathers. None of those who despised Me will see it" (Num. 14:21ff). Caleb believed in the promises of God, however, and did not waver in his conviction that the Israelites could take the land in the power of God. Because of his faithful belief in the promise of God, God rewarded Caleb. "Since my servant Caleb has a different spirit and followed Me completely, I will bring him into the land where he has gone, and his descendants will inherit it" (Num. 14:24).

Caleb persevered in the promises of God, and the account of the reception of his reward is recorded in Joshua 14:13–14. Caleb further demonstrated his trust in God by requesting the land occupied by the *giants* of the lands, the Anakites. He appealed to the promises of God to enable him to drive out the Anakites and take the land. "Now give me this hill country the Lord promised me on that day, because you heard then that the Anakim are there, as well as large fortified cities. Perhaps the Lord will be with me and I will drive them out as the Lord promised" (Josh. 14:12). This biblical text connects the ability to persevere with the ability to confront and overcome the obstacles of life. The reality of the faithfulness of God shapes and supports our ability to persevere in the course of life, even when great obstacles and barriers appear to impede our path. Sometimes God will equip us to conquer "the giants" of our lives. Sometimes God will equip to continue to wait until He removes the *giants* of our lives. In either of these cases, God will work in us in such a way that we can successfully persevere through life.

Conclusion

The writer of Ecclesiastes stated: "The end of a matter is better than its beginning; a patient spirit is better than a proud spirit" (Eccl. 7:8). This verse underscores the truth that how we conclude the race of our life is more important than how we begin that race. As one preacher once remarked, "In the Christian life, how you finish is more important than how you start." Caleb models the importance of this biblical truth. The Christian life is one marked by perseverance. In His grace and mercy, God provides His Holy Spirit to instill and work within each believer the disposition of perseverance. Perseverance thereby becomes one of the tenets, or fruits, that distinguish us as a regenerate child of God. The work of God whereby He sustains and equips us to finish the race of our life is called perseverance. Let us therefore persevere with excellence in the race of life in which our Heavenly Father has placed each of us.

R. Stanton Norman serves as the Vice President for University Relations at Southwest Baptist University. He holds a BA from Criswell College, and the MDiv and PhD from Southwestern Baptist Theological Seminary.

Part II
A Matter of Worldview

Devotions and Essays on a Biblical Worldview

- Marketing, Management, Technology and Entrepreneurship
- Competition, Success, and Ethics
- Accounting, Finance, and Economics
- Leadership and Motivation

9

Marketing, Management, and Technology

"You will always reap what you sow!
Those who live only to satisfy their own sinful desires
will harvest the consequences of decay and death.
But those who live to please the Spirit
will harvest everlasting life from the Spirit."
—Gal. 6:7–8

"If you ignore criticism, you will end in poverty and disgrace;
if you accept criticism, you will be honored."
—Prov. 13:18 NLT

"Therefore, my beloved brethren, be ye steadfast, unmovable,
always abounding in the work of the Lord,
orasmuch as ye know that your labour
is not in vain in the Lord."
—1 Cor. 15:58 KJV

"When one door of opportunity closes, another opens;
but often we look so long at the closed door
that we do not see the one which has been opened for us."
—Helen Keller

"Every man is born into the world to do something unique
and something distinctive, and if he or she does not do it,
it will never be done."
—Benjamin Mays

"God grant me the serenity
to accept the things I cannot change,
courage to change the things I can,
and wisdom to know the difference."
—Reinhold Niebuhr

"Opportunity is missed by most people
because it comes dressed in overalls and looks like work."
—Thomas Edison

"Never discourage anyone who continually makes progress,
no matter how slow."
—Plato

"Those are weaklings who know the truth and uphold it
as long it suits their purpose, and then abandon it."
—Blaise Pascal

"I expect to pass through the world but once. Any good therefore that I can do, or any kindness I can show to any creature, let me do it now. Let me not defer it, for I shall not pass this way again."
—Stephen Grellet

"Hold yourself responsible for a higher standard
than anyone else expects of you. Never excuse yourself."
—Henry Ward Beecher

Redeemed Marketing

Julie Huntley and David Dyson

Marketing and Christianity, what could they possibly have in common? For many, marketing is a secular—perhaps even vulgar word—a necessary evil for businesses wanting to make a profit. Marketing may be seen as manipulative and deceptive—simply a way to make people buy a product. Consequently, how can marketing be used by Christians in good conscience? Are not marketers little more than *shysters*? While many unscrupulous practices have certainly been evident in marketing, to limit the nature and scope of marketing to these negative manifestations is a mistake. To dismiss marketing as unholy because of deception and manipulation would be comparable to declaring Christianity as unholy because of the backsliders and charlatans frequently found within its borders.

It is incumbent upon Christian professionals to clarify these misconceptions and demonstrate the benefits of good marketing. Important to note for Christians, this redeemed marketing can be practiced ethically and with good conscience. It can result in value for *all* involved while offering win-win solutions. To begin this discussion, prior descriptions of what marketing has been will be analyzed to understand its transformation into contemporary practice. Building on this foundation, further discussion of its value within a Christian worldview will be developed.

Marketing Defined

In general, if one were to ask his/her neighbor or work colleague to define marketing, they would probably mention some aspect of selling or advertising. Since most people have been exposed to a great deal of advertising or have been the target of selling efforts (some of the most visible aspects of marketing), definitions for marketing are typically limited to these boundaries. In reality, however, the scope of marketing extends far beyond these two activities and has evolved as a reflection of successful business practices over time.

Part II: A Matter of Worldview

This progression of marketing activity has been categorized into four *eras* of marketing. These eras suggest prevailing attitudes and approaches to marketing that were successful under certain market conditions. Adjusting to the conditions of various time periods, "successful" marketing practices emerged. A discussion of these eras offers insight into what works and what doesn't work, to more readily determine current application for Christians. One of the first eras was the *production era*.

The prevailing attitude of the *production era* (generally considered prior to the 1920s) was that a good product will sell itself. If marketers designed and built a great product, sales volume would increase (supply-side economics) as a result of customers lining up to purchase the product. At that time, when demand exceeded supply, this approach to marketing was effective. However, as supply began to exceed demand, the *sales era* came into existence (generally considered prior to the 1950s). The prevailing attitude of the sales era was that consumers are resistant to efforts to sell a product. Marketers must use creative advertising and selling gimmicks to overcome this resistance and thereby increase sales volume.

Following World War II, marketers recognized the growing sophistication of consumers and the abundant supply of products. The prevailing attitude of the *marketing era* (generally since the 1950s) became the "consumer is king." One must find a need and fill it to be successful. Known as the marketing concept, increased sales would result from customer and need satisfaction. Currently, in the *relationship era* of marketing (since the 1990s), businesses have identified the importance of not only implementing the marketing concept (i.e., meeting needs of customers), but also of developing long-term relationships with customers and business partners to be successful in the marketplace.

While approaches from all of these eras are evident in the contemporary environment, to be successful in current market conditions, businesses must maintain relationships with customers through need satisfaction to achieve long-term success. Organizations focused on producing great, quality products (production era) without a focus on customer needs can enjoy only limited success. Organizations focused on creative advertising and selling (sales era) without considering customer needs, may experience increased sales; however, with little focus on customer retention, the sales may be short-lived. Considering the high costs of acquiring new customers (approximately five times that of retaining customers), the ability to retain existing customers through need fulfillment and customer satisfaction is far more desirable and cost-effective in the long-run.

From these practices, a shift in focus is evident. The focus switched from self (what one produces) to customer (what need may be satisfied). A singular focus on me and my product and what selling techniques *I* can implement to fulfill needs is a narrow focus that will limit success. The key to successful marketing strategy is to start with the people (customers) and remain focused on people (customers)! By identifying and satisfying people's needs, relationships are formed and sustained. Personal and organizational objectives are then addressed and mutual rewards are achieved.

Thus, in contemporary markets, business success is achieved by focusing externally on the needs of others. A shortsighted, narrow, internal focus on my capabilities, resources, and objectives will not achieve optimal success, long-term. With the explication of these fundamental marketing concepts in mind, the issue of marketing and its alignment with Christian values can now be addressed. Responses to the questions: "Is marketing ethically and morally sound?" and "Does the Bible support its practice?" can be determined.

Marketing Practice with a Christian Worldview

Based on the prior discussion of needs-based and benefit-based marketing, the alignment with Christian values is clearly supported. Focused on need satisfaction, it has been said that marketing is about making life better. This is completely consistent with Jesus' mission (John 10:10). Christianity, of course, is centered on serving others (Matt. 23:11). Serving others, fundamentally, is about meeting needs. Since God desires to meet all of our needs (Phil.4:19), marketing can actually be a reflection of His character. With its love focus, Christian motives and actions are based on addressing the interests of others over one's own in a servant leadership model (1 Cor. 13:5; 10:24).

For Christians, motives are a key issue for sound marketing. Are the motives based in self-interest where selfish desires are to increase patronage and profit at someone else's expense? Or, are the motives based in serving others where the desires are to do what is right and fulfill their needs most effectively with God's resources? Right motives are clearly consistent with right marketing!

When further considering the value of marketing and its alignment with biblical principles, a fair question to ask is: "Can the Great Commission be fulfilled in a world void of marketing?" A fundamental activity of Christianity is witnessing—promotion at its finest! Two forms of promotion are personal selling and advertising. In the Great Commission,

Christians are actually commanded to go into all the world and preach the gospel to all creation (Mark 16: 15). When witnessing, Christians communicate verbally (personal selling) or through their lifestyle (advertising) the message of the gospel with the objective of informing, influencing, and persuading people to make a decision for Jesus Christ. Christians' lives are actually living promotion for Christ.

To complete this analogy with the additional Ps of the marketing mix since promotion is outlined above, the product (or service) might be considered salvation. While the price for salvation was paid by Jesus, Christians must give their lives as submitted vessels to the Lord. Distribution (place) includes the entire world since salvation is available to all. Consequently, not only is marketing consistent with godly values, it is used as a primary tool in the spreading of the gospel! Christianity is about meeting spiritual, physical, financial, and social needs of people. Marketing, therefore, seems to not only align well with Christian values but to actually be an effective tool for ministry. As with any tool, a tool can be used correctly or it can be abused. These abuses have been evident not only in the business world but the ministerial world as well, with deceptive and manipulative practices. However, marketing as a practice is not inherently wrong and seems to be strongly supported by biblical principles and practice.

What does this suggest for Christian marketers? In the twenty-first century, a new standard in character is emerging for business professionals. The crisis of confidence and trust in leaders and corporations is forcing a re-evaluation of ethical standards. As companies are being held to higher standards, character is being sought in new college graduates. The mandate is clear. Practice good (redeemed) marketing with Christian values. Customer-driven, moral business is good business. Sound marketing and Christian principles go hand in hand. As Christians, marketers can practice sound marketing with Christian character and experience God's blessing on their businesses. New standards—His standards—can be set, resulting in marketing practices filled with His favor and blessing.

Julie Huntley serves as Associate Professor of Marketing at Oral Roberts University. She holds a BSBA from the University of Nebraska, an MBA from Oral Roberts University and the PhD from Arizona State University.

David Dyson serves as Professor of Business at Oral Roberts University, and previously served as the Dean of the School of Business for nine years. He earned both his BA and MBA at Oral Roberts University and his PhD at the University of Arkansas.

Under New Management

Ronda O. Credille

Under New Management

Reading one of these signs at a place of business always piques my curiosity. Did the previous manager leave voluntarily? Was the new manager promoted from within the firm? How will the employees relate to the new manager? Will the new manager be an improvement over the old one?

Hailed by *Business Week* as "The Man Who Invented Management,"[1] Peter Drucker once said, "So much of what we call management consists in making it difficult for people to work." Can management from a biblical worldview make a difference? After only one class session in Principles of Management, a student should be able to recite the four basic functions of management: Planning, Organizing, Leading, and Controlling. Examples of the application of each of these functions can be found in Scripture.

Planning

The planning function of management involves establishing a mission, developing goals, creating strategies, and making decisions. Planning is an ongoing process. Plans must be reviewed regularly and revised or changed as needed. Plans are categorized based on their purpose and use. Strategic plans are relatively long-term in nature, are based on the mission of the organization and include the goals and objectives the organization desires to achieve. Operational (or tactical) plans give more details as to how the goals and objectives will be reached. Plans that are used repeatedly are known as standing plans; a customized plan for a specific situation is called a *single-use* plan. Plans may simply provide general guidelines (directional plans), but sometimes plans must be so specific as to allow for no deviation at all.

---

1. Byrne, J. A. (2005). "The Man Who Invented Management." *Business Week Online.* Retrieved March 25, 2007 from http://www.businessweek.com/magazine/content/05_48/b3961001.htm.

Jehovah God's strategic plan was to establish an everlasting covenant with Abraham and his descendants where they would worship and serve Him in the land of Canaan (Gen. 17:4–8). Many operational plans were implemented between the time of Abraham and the time of the Exodus to guide the Israelites back to the covenant. Following their departure from Egypt, the Lord instructed Moses to build a tabernacle so that He could dwell among the people of Israel. The construction plans the Lord provided to Moses were highly detailed; these plans would be classified as *specific* and *single-use*. The Lord ordered the building of the tabernacle that He "might dwell with them" (Exod. 25:8 NIV). King Solomon, to whom Jehovah gave more wisdom than any other human being, provides guidelines for planning in the book of Proverbs. Solomon addresses the role of godly wisdom and the importance of planning, seeking advice and maintaining one's core values.

The Role of Godly Wisdom

Solomon declares that wisdom begins with the fear of the Lord (Prov. 9:10 NIV). Amazingly, though "wisdom is more precious than rubies," the Father gives it away (Prov. 8:11; 2:6 NIV). Solomon proclaims that wisdom will not only protect and watch over us (Prov. 4:6 NIV), but will save us from falling prey to corrupt individuals (Prov. 2:12 NIV). Corporate scandals have become almost a routine occurrence in the modern business world. Christian business people would do well to pray for wisdom daily as they make important decisions. Regular doses of prayer and godly wisdom would significantly reduce our susceptibility to unethical people and schemes.

The Importance of Planning

Solomon states, "The plans of the diligent lead to profit as surely as haste leads to poverty" (Prov. 21:5 NIV). The conclusion is clear: thorough, conscientious planning quite literally pays! By contrast, sketchy plans or careless actions can spell the death knell for an organization. The late Bob Briner, former president of ProServ Television, wrote, "A fundamental management principle, for both individuals and for organizations, is to have a plan to which you are deeply committed, and then set out with determination to accomplish it."[2] As good stewards of an organization's assets, careful planning is essential. Jesus gave the example of how foolish

---

2. Briner, B. (1996). *The Management Methods of Jesus: Ancient Wisdom for Modern Business.* Nashville, Tennessee: Thomas Nelson, Inc., pp. 1–2.

it would be for a person wanting to build a tower *not* to have a financial plan to complete it. The adage, failing to plan is planning to fail, has great merit. Financial failure due to poor planning can quickly damage the credibility—and therefore, witness—of a Christian businessperson.

The Importance of Seeking Advice

Solomon bluntly states in Proverbs, "The way of a fool seems right to him, but a wise man listens to advice" (Prov. 12:15 NIV). A more diplomatic statement reads, "Plans fail for lack of counsel, but with many advisers they succeed" (Prov. 15:22 NIV). For those rugged individualists who think they always know best, Solomon warns, "Pride only breeds quarrels, but wisdom is found in those who take advice" (Prov. 13:10 NIV). Max DePree, former CEO of Herman Miller, Inc., said, "I believe that the most effective contemporary management process is participative management."[3] DePree asserts that "everyone has the right and duty to influence decision making and to understand the results."[4] A wise manager will seek the advice of employees who will be affected by the manager's decisions. The responsibility of the decision still rests with the manager, but employees can provide important perspectives not yet considered by the manager.

Maintaining Your Core Values

Repeatedly, Solomon admonishes his readers to remember and to live by the values their parents had instilled in them. One example of these admonitions is: "Keep your father's commands and do not forsake your mother's teaching" (Prov. 6:20 NIV). DePree declares, "Our value system and worldview should be as closely integrated into our work lives as they are integrated into our lives with our families, our churches and our other activities. . . ."[5] John D. Beckett, chairman of R. W. Beckett Corporation, led managers in their multiple business units to develop a document that outlined the corporation's "vision, mission, core values and governing principles."[6] The standards in this document (dubbed their *Corporate Roadmap*) were communicated to every employee. According to Beckett,

---

3. DePree, M. (1987). *Leadership is an Art.* East Lansing, Michigan: Michigan State University Press, p. 24.

4. Ibid.

5. Ibid., p. 26.

6. Beckett, J. (2006). *Mastering Monday: A Guide to Integrating Faith and Work.* Downers Grove, Illinois: Intervarsity Press Books. p. 31.

these written standards have been invaluable in "defining and sustaining the business culture" in their various businesses.[7]

Organizing

The management function of organizing is concerned with the allocation of resources. Interrogatives such as what, who, how, and where are addressed by this function. In the tabernacle example, the Lord listed the materials that were needed for its construction; who was to donate them; how they were to be used and where each component of the tabernacle's furnishings was to be placed. The Lord even designated which craftsmen were to take lead positions in the construction. God had given Bezalel the "skill, ability and knowledge" to perform the "artistic craftsmanship" (Exod. 35:30, 33 NIV). God had also given Bezalel and Oholiab "the ability to teach others . . . to do all kinds of work as craftsmen, designers," etc. (Exod. 35:35). This example illustrates the need to carefully match the abilities of the employee to the task.

The account of Bezalel and Oholiab also highlights the use of a training technique comparable to today's mentoring relationships. Mentoring pairs a new employee with an experienced one "who provides information, support, and encouragement."[8] John Beckett reports that R. W. Beckett Corporation managers, "are specifically trained to 'serve' their employees: facilitating, not demanding; coaching, not bossing; teaching, not criticizing."[9] Business expert and best-selling author Tom Peters says, "Leaders don't create followers, they create more leaders."[10] Jehovah selected Joshua to become the protégé of Moses (Num. 27:18–20). When Moses died at age 120, Joshua was ready to assume command of the Israelite people (Deut. 34:9). Moses had served well as Joshua's mentor.

One aspect of organizing is determining the appropriate span of control for managers. This concept can be traced back to Jethro, Moses' father-in-law, who observed that Moses was exhausted from serving as the judge for every dispute that arose among the Israelites. With his father-in-law's guidance, Moses learned how to delegate. Moses organized the people into "thousands, hundreds, fifties, and tens" and appointed

---

7. Ibid, p. 32.

8. Robbins, S. and Coulter, M. (2005). *Management, 8e.* Upper Saddle River, New Jersey: Pearson-Prentice Hall, p. 295.

9. Becket, J. (1998). *Loving Monday: Succeeding in Business Without Selling Your Soul.* Downers Grove, Illinois: Intervarsity Press Books, p. 119.

10. Retrieved March 25, 2007 from http://www.quotegarden.com/leadershiop.html.

"capable men . . . who fear[ed] God" and were trustworthy to serve as "leaders of the people" (Exod. 18:21 NIV).

Jethro also advised Moses that the implementation of the assistant judge system should be preceded by training sessions for the Israelite people in order to reduce the number of conflicts for which a judge was needed. Moses was to "teach them the decrees and laws, and show them the way to live and the duties they [were] to perform" (Exod. 18:20). Jethro supplied the job specifications for the position of assistant judge. A job specification "identifies the knowledge, skills, and attitudes needed to do the job effectively."[11] Moses was to consider only those individuals who were capable, trustworthy and ethical (Exod. 18:21). Even if a person possessed the required knowledge or skills, an individual who was untrustworthy, had a reputation for accepting bribes, or had cheated others was automatically disqualified from consideration. Robbins and Coulter define trust as "the belief in the integrity, character, and ability of a leader."[12] Furthermore, Robbins and Coulter declare that "followers judge a leader's credibility in terms of his or her honesty, competence, and ability to inspire."[13] When it comes to allocating human resources, only individuals who have demonstrated trustworthiness should be elevated to positions of authority.

Leading

Directing the work of others and motivating them to achieve the organization's objectives are components of the leading function of management. The late President Dwight D. Eisenhower said that leadership is, "the art of getting someone else to do something you want done because he wants to do it."[14] In Exodus, God reveals to Moses that He has chosen him to lead the Israelites out of Egyptian slavery and into "a good and spacious land . . . flowing with milk and honey" (Exod. 3:8–10 NIV). To call Moses a reluctant leader would be an understatement. Despite his professed shortcomings, however, God used Moses to accomplish amazing feats during the next forty years before his death at the age of 120. Moses coordinated the migration of as many as two million people; received and interpreted God's Laws for Israelites; authored, under divine inspiration, the first five books of the Old Testament and at least one Psalm (Ps. 90);

---

11. Robbins, S. and Coulter, M. (2005). *Management, 8e.* Upper Saddle River, New Jersey: Pearson-Prentice Hall, p. 286.
12. Ibid., p. 438.
13. Ibid.
14. Retrieved March 25, 2007 from http://www.quotegarden.com/leadership.html.

supervised the building of the tabernacle; interceded with Jehovah to spare the lives of the Israelites numerous times; and assembled an army that God used to defeat the Midianites.

Moses is described as the most humble man on earth in Numbers 12:3. Considering that the authorship of Numbers is attributed to Moses, one might well wonder why he would say that about himself if he were so humble![15] Dr. William Smith offers a possible explanation of this seeming incongruity.[16] The context of this verse is the occasion when Miriam and Aaron openly opposed their brother Moses. In the remainder of the passage, the Lord defends Moses, and declares, "With [Moses], I speak face to face" (Num. 12:8 NIV). Moses did not seek to be the leader of the Israelites. In fact, according to Exodus 4:13–14, Moses would have gleefully turned the entire assignment over to Aaron—or anyone else, for that matter—if the Lord had not pressed Moses into service. Dr. H. I. Hester interprets the word *humble* (or *meek*, in the King James Version) as "unselfish disinterestedness."[17] This interpretation is consistent with Smith's explanation. Smith observes that Moses, "always forgot himself when the good of his people was to be served."[18] In his book, *A Dangerous Grace*, Charles Colson contends, "Those who accept the biblical view of servant leadership treat power as a humbling delegation from God, not as a right to control others."[19]

In the book they co-authored, Charles Colson and Jack Eckerd defined servant leadership as: "doing our very best for others."[20] DePree identifies the ability to "lead through serving" as one of the chief "traits that should be present in all leaders."[21] The merit of this quality is even recognized by secular experts. Robert Swiggert, former president and CEO of Kollmorgen (a manufacturer of military and aerospace equipment), was quoted by *Inc.* magazine as saying, "The role of the leader is a servant's

---

15. Note: Some scholars think that this verse was added to the text at a later time to provide readers with an explanation as to how unjust Miriam and Aaron were in their opposition to Moses. *NIV Study Bible* (1995).

16. Smith, W. *Smith's Bible Dictionary*. Philadelphia: A.J. Holman Company. p. 208.

17. Hester, H. I. (1962). *The Heart of Hebrew History*. Liberty, Missouri: The Quality Press, p. 136.

18. Smith, W. *Smith's Bible Dictionary*. Philadelphia: A.J. Holman Company. p. 208.

19. Colson, C. with Pearcey, N. (1994). *A Dangerous Grace*. Dallas, Texas: Word Publishing, p. 112.

20. Colson, C. A & Eckerd, J. (1991). *Why America Doesn't Work*. Dallas, Texas: Word Publishing, p. 168.

21. DePree, M. (1987). *Leadership is an Art*. East Lansing, Michigan: Michigan State University Press, p. 125.

role."[22] Humility is a prerequisite for genuine servant leadership. Briner remarks that if he senses the genesis of arrogance within himself, he resists it by calling to mind the image of Jesus Christ kneeling before His disciples and washing their feet.[23]

The Apostle Paul instructed believers not to think of themselves more highly than they should (Rom. 12:3). He did not mean that believers should have *low* self-esteem—just a proper estimation of their worth from God's perspective. In *Business by the Book*, the late Larry Burkett (founder of Christian Financial Concepts) listed six "Basic Biblical Minimums" for Christians in business, one of which was "Treat Your Employees Fairly."[24] Fair treatment begins with recognizing that "all people are important, regardless of income or education."[25] Burkett stated, "One of the best things you can do to ensure a good working environment and even improve the bottom line is to display and encourage respect for others."[26] DePree affirms that belief: "[I]t is fundamental that leaders endorse a concept of persons."[27] A leader's demonstration of respect for others is crucial. As Albert Schweitzer said, "Example is not the main thing in influencing others. It is the only thing."[28]

Controlling

The seeds of the controlling function of management are sown in the planning phase when the standards of performance are established. The purpose of the control function is to ensure that the organization stays on track to meet its goals. Control in this application of the word is not synonymous with manipulate or coerce. The first step in the control process is to measure the performance outcomes. This information can be acquired through reports (oral, written or statistical) or observations. The second step is to compare the actual performance to the established standard(s). If

---

22. *Inc.* (1984, April) quoted in Peters, T. & Austin, N. (1985). *A Passion for Excellence*. New York: Warner Books, Inc., p. 240.

23. Ibid., p. 36.

24. Burkett, L. (1998). *Business by The Book*. Nashville, Tennessee: Thomas Nelson Publishing, p. 19.

25. Ibid., p. 20.

26. Ibid., p. 105.

27. DePree, M. (1987). *Leadership is an Art*. East Lansing, Michigan: Michigan State University Press, p. 9.

28. Retrieved March 31, 2007 from http://quotations.about.com/od/stillmorefamouspeople/a/AlbertSchweitz1.htm.

a significant deviation exists, adjustments may need to be made. Examples of control measures that are used by businesses are budgets and product defect rates.

Moses relied on a combination of oral reports, personal observations and written reports to monitor and evaluate the performance of the Israelites. After forty days of fasting and praying on Mount Sinai, he came down to the Israelite camp only to see the people committing multiple violations of the very Ten Commandments he had just received from Jehovah! During his forty years as their leader, Moses reminded the people through frequent addresses that obedience to God would bring blessings and prosperity, but disobedience would result in curses and destruction (e.g., Deut. 30:15–18). He completed a written version of God's law and gave it to the priests shortly before his death (Deut. 31:9). He instructed the Levites to read the law to the entire nation every seven years to remind them of the standards that Jehovah had set for them (Deut. 31:10–12).

Several important lessons about control can be gleaned from the experiences of Moses. Standards should be written and widely disseminated to the people who must follow them. Frequent verbal reminders of expectations should be given. Performance should be documented and reviewed regularly. Achievements should be rewarded. The manager should be visible and accessible to the subordinates. Tom Peters defines control as, "the knowledge that someone who is interested and cares is paying close attention."[29] Peters and Robert H. Waterman, Jr. popularized the idea of *Management by Wandering Around* (MBWA) in their book *In Search of Excellence*, published in 1982. The authors were inspired by the "tribal storytellers"[30] at Hewlett-Packard who told of co-founder Dave Packard's management technique, "which [was] marked by personal involvement, good listening skills and the recognition that 'everyone in an organization wants to do a good job.'"[31]

In *The Management Methods of Jesus*, Briner charged managers to "evaluate constantly."[32] Briner suggested that the only way to ensure that employees have accurately comprehended the company's mission and

29. Peters, T. & Austin, N. (1985). *A passion for excellence.* New York: Warner Books, Inc., p. 370.

30. DePree, M. (1987). *Leadership is an Art.* East Lansing, Michigan: Michigan State University Press, p. 84.

31. Retrieved March 29, 2007 from http://www.hp.com/hpinfo/abouthp/histnfacts/timeline/hist_40s.html.

32. Briner, B. (1996). *The Management Methods of Jesus: Ancient Wisdom for Modern Business.* Nashville, Tennessee: Thomas Nelson, Inc., p. 97.

goals is to continuously ask them questions. Briner stated, "By asking questions and having your people articulate the answers, you will be able to determine the extent of their understanding and identify the areas that need to be retaught."[33]

Making a Difference

Is the practice of management destined to make "it difficult for people to work," as Drucker observed? Not if the management is based on a biblical worldview. This philosophy of management relies on godly wisdom and prudent advice when planning. Biblical management requires honesty, integrity, and trust when organizing resources. A servant leader is one who "enables others to reach their potential" while exemplifying humility, respecting all persons equally and doing what is in the best interest of the organization.[34] Control from a biblical perspective means holding members of the organization accountable while simultaneously letting them know that someone is concerned about their performance and is "paying close attention."[35] Management based on a biblical worldview, according to DePree, "liberate[s] people to do what is required of them in the most effective and humane way possible"[36]

Can someone who is neither the organization's CEO nor an executive make a difference? John Beckett explains how God can use people to "influence the future of [their] company."[37] Beckett provides an example of an individual who accomplished this task because he "earned respect in his sphere of responsibility…cared for the whole company, not just his own bailiwick; . . . [and] approached this difficult assignment prayerfully and respectfully."[38]

When "confronted by the old battle between the marketplace and ministry," as Beckett describes it in *Mastering Monday*,[39] remember two

---

33. Ibid.

34. DePree, M. (1987). *Leadership is an Art*. East Lansing, Michigan: Michigan State University Press, p. 19.

35. Peters, T. & Austin, N. (1985). *A Passion for Excellence*. New York: Warner Books, Inc., p. 370.

36. DePree, M. (1987). *Leadership is an Art*. East Lansing, Michigan: Michigan State University Press, p. xx.

37. Beckett, J. (2006). *Mastering Monday: A Guide to Integrating Faith and Work*. Downers Grove, Illinois: Intervarsity Press Books, p. 71.

38. Ibid.

39. Ibid, p. 28.

verses from the writings of the Apostle Paul: "Whatever you do, do it all for the glory of God . . . Whether in word or deed, do it all in the name of the Lord Jesus, giving thanks to God the Father through Him" (1 Cor. 10:31; Col. 3:17). Christians should manage consistent with this scripture. After all, the believer is under new management as well!

Ronda O. Credille is an Associate Professor of Business Administration at Southwest Baptist University. She holds a BS from Southwest Baptist University, an MBA from Drury College and the PhD from the University of Nebraska.

Of Heroes and Managers

Phillip V. Lewis, Dean

A LYRICAL lament of country music legend Willie Nelson is "Where have all the heroes gone?" Many individuals ask that same question. Who can blame them with what an increasingly cynical media places before the public. The truth is: Not all the heroes are missing from action. You can find many of them working in nonprofit organizations, in government, in community organizations, and in business. Their numbers will multiply as Christian leaders help bring those whom they lead under the transformational power of God, as all then become (for sake of better terminology) *transformational leaders*.[40]

Transformation is a converting process. Managerial leaders change (or convert) from one style of thinking or acting to another style of thinking or acting. Realistically, however, no organization can be transformed unless the mind sets of those involved are changed. Change is an attitude or a state of mind. In many respects, the internal constituents are the most crucial parts of the organization and the most critical to the change process.[41] Yet, the way of doing things (i.e., the system) often is easier to change than the people. Peter Drucker has written, "The final requirement of effective leadership is to earn trust. Otherwise there won't be any followers. . . . A leader is someone who has followers. To trust a leader, it is not necessary to agree with him. Trust is the conviction that leaders mean what they say. It is a belief in something very old-fashioned called integrity."

Benjamin Franklin said, "It is a grand mistake to think of being great without goodness; and I pronounce it as certain that there was never yet a truly great man that was not at the same time truly virtuous." Henry

---

40. Several of the ideas in this paper were adapted from James Patterson and Peter Kim, *The Day America Told the Truth* (New York: Prentice Hall Press, 1991); Sylvia Nash, "Living with Integrity in A Chaotic World," a speech presented to the Christian Business Faculty Association, Azusa Pacific University, October 7, 1994; Phillip V. Lewis, *Transformational Leadership: A New Model for Total Church Involvement* (Nashville: Broadman & Holman, 1996); R. Bruce Hutton, "Where Have All the Heroes Gone?" *Daniels Business Review*, Winter 1997, pp. 2–9.

41. See Romans 12:1–8; 1 Corinthians 12; and Ephesians 4:11–13.

David Thoreau penned, "How often must one feel as he looks back on his past life that he has gained a talent but lost a character. . . . Society does nominally estimate men by their talents, but really feels and knows them by their character." Unfortunately, our world seems to have lost its emphasis on integrity, considering it to no longer be an issue for political leaders. However, Richard Breedan, former chairman of the SEC once stated, It is not an adequate ethical standard to aspire to get through the day without being indicted." Charley Reese, a newspaper columnist, celebrated the birthday of George Washington by writing: "What distinguished Washington, aside from his courage and competence, was his integrity. A British historian said of him, 'In Washington, America found a leader who could be induced by no earthy motive to tell a falsehood, or to break an engagement or to commit any dishonorable act.'" [42]

"Thomas Jefferson once said, regarding Washington, 'He errs as other men do, but errs with integrity.' An artist, Gilbert Stuart, remarked . . . 'All his features are indicative of the strongest passions; yet his judgment and great self-command make him appear a man of a different cast in the eyes of the world.'"[43] Is it possible to find such leaders and managers today? Yes, but the search for them is sometimes frustrating. According to 1,300 senior executives who responded to a survey, integrity is the human quality most necessary to business success; seventy-one percent put it at the top of a list of sixteen traits responsible for enhancing an executive's effectiveness. Yet, according to a Gallup poll of business executives, we live in a world where:

- 80% admit to driving while drunk.
- 35% overstate tax deductions.
- 75% take work supplies for personal use.
- 78% use the company phone for personal long distance calls.

A study by the Office of Technology Assessment determined that 33% of the U.S. government's telephone bill is spent on personal calls. General Motors reported losing 9% of employee hours due to absenteeism. White-collar crime in the U.S. is estimated at $40 billion per year. The Bible sets forth Ten Commandments for people to follow; however, it is estimated that U.S. legislators have passed 35 million laws designed to enforce those Ten Commandments. Only 13% of the U.S. population feels the Ten Commandments have relevance. Yet, Americans feel the number one cause of business decline is low executive ethics. A survey

---

42. Charley Reese, "Washington was Nation's Indispensable Man," *San Gabriel Valley Tribune,* February 22, 1998, p. A17.

43. Ibid.

conducted by *Personnel Journal* of Costa Mesa, California, found that middle managers, aged 40–45 are more likely than other employees to be dishonest because of the intense pressure to get ahead. People midway through their careers are the ones most likely to steal, bend the truth, and cheat on their expense accounts.

James Patterson and Peter Kim conducted a survey of more than 2,000 Americans over a one-week period of time. Those surveyed were given the opportunity to express what they believed about things that mattered. Each of them answered over 1800 questions. Thousands more answered a shorter version of the questionnaire or cooperated in telephone interviews. It is one of the most massive in-depth surveys to be conducted of what Americans really believe. Here are some of the highlights of that study:

- 68% don't believe America has a single hero right now.
- 80% believe morals and ethics should be taught in the nation's schools again.
- 90% said they truly believed in God; yet when they make decisions on right and wrong, they do not turn to God or religion for help.
- Women are morally superior to men. They lie less, are more responsible and far more honest at work, and can be trusted more. (These factors were the conclusions of both men and women.)
- 50% of high school students and 30% of college students cheat on exams. (A study by the Institute of Ethics found that these students believe, "it is not unethical to do whatever you have to do to succeed if you don't seriously hurt other people.")
- 30% of high school students lie on their job application.
- 20% of students falsify reports to keep their jobs. Worse yet, their parents are the examples they are following. (The Josephson Institute of Ethics says that many Americans ache to do the right thing but feel there are no outlets through our current institutions.)

A cartoon in the *New Yorker Magazine* depicted two clean-shaven middle-aged men sitting in a jail cell. One inmate turns to the other and says: "All along, I thought our level of corruption fell well within community standards." In the book, *The Day America Told the Truth*, various professions were graded for integrity. Firemen were No. 1, Catholic priests were No. 7, college professors were No. 10, and Protestant ministers were No. 19. The president of the U.S. rated No. 28, which is a notch below the average plumber and construction worker. The TV evangelist was No. 69, which was third from the bottom, barely nosing out drug dealers and

Part II: A Matter of Worldview

crime bosses. But those three (TV evangelists, drug dealers, and crime bosses) failed to match the moral standards of prostitutes.[44]

Robert Bork's book, *Slouching Towards Gomorrah*, "offers a prophetic and unprecedented view of a culture in decline, a nation in such serious moral trouble that its very foundation is crumbling."[45] He describes America as "a monster of decadence, a plague several generations in gestation" and cites that "we are now slouching, not towards Bethlehem . . . but towards Gomorrah, the biblical city burned to the ground for the sinfulness of its people."[46] If organizations and the people who work inside them are to be transformed, managerial leaders have a tremendous challenge. Yet, if there is any group who ought to be able to make a difference in this mixed up world, where Elvis is alive and God is dead, it is those individuals. They have the unique challenge of transforming a world in which integrity seems to be a thing of the past.

Today, as never before, communities are looking to its business and civic leaders. What leaders do speaks so loudly that people can't hear what they're saying! One's personal integrity is at center stage for all to see—or hear. They will never be able to transform others or organizations if they themselves have not been transformed—if their integrity is questionable. Concerning the first president, George Washington, Charley Reese also wrote:

> The narcotic effect of power, fame and adulation had no effect on him. . . . Daniel Webster said, 'If nothing else, America can always be proud of Washington.' Few, if any, humans can be said to be indispensable, but Washington probably was. There were others who could have handled the political chores of the Revolution, but they could not have held together the ragged army that ultimately defeated the British. No one else could have welded the federalists and the republicans into one administration. No one else could have assured ratification of the Constitution simply by endorsing it."[47]

In a day and time when "There are few people . . . worth reading about, though it is commonplace for entertainers and non-entities to write autobiographies and memoirs," it is nice to know that once our nation had

---

44. James Patterson & Peter Kim, *The Day America Told the Truth: What People Really Believe About Everything That Really Matters* (New York: Prentice Hall Press, 1991).

45. Robert Bork, *Slouching Towards Gomorrah: Modern Liberalism and American Decline* (New York: The Free Press, 1997).

46. Ibid.

47. Charley Reese, "Washington was Nation's Indispensable Man," *San Gabriel Valley Tribune*, February 22, 1998, p. A17.

an "indispensable man."[48] The Bible sets forth a story about another man of integrity, Daniel. "Now Daniel so distinguished himself among the administrators . . . of his exceptional qualities that the king planned to set him over the whole kingdom. At this the administrators . . . tried to find grounds for charges against Daniel in his conduct of government affairs, but they were unable to do so. They could find no corruption in him, because he was trustworthy and neither corrupt nor negligent" (Dan. 6:3–5).

Today's business organizations and communities still need a George Washington and a Daniel, leaders who are trustworthy and neither corrupt nor negligent—leaders on whom the narcotic effect of power, fame, and adulation have no effect. Communities, businesses, and agencies still need integrity! Managerial leaders need to be the transformational leaders who can help bring about these needed changes. Heroes are still needed who operate with the highest degree of integrity, provide quality and personal service, build meaningful relationships, and get involved in assuring healthy communities. Transformational leaders are still needed! If a managerial leader wishes to transform those with whom he or she works and the organization, she/he must first transform self and bring that life under God's rule. At the core of that transformation is an utterly simple idea—a belief in something very old-fashioned called *integrity*. One must live and manage with integrity before anyone else will want to be a follower and place himself or herself under another's leadership!

Finally, believers who manage with integrity do not fail to shine their lights; they do not hide their lights under a bushel. Believing managers and leaders are those who have been delivered from darkness into His wonderful light that we might declare His praises. God's Light has indeed come into the world. Hide not your light by failing to live and manage with integrity. Become the transformational leader God desires. The world is looking for heroes. Perhaps through your leadership position, they'll find someone worth emulating. Perhaps they'll find the One worth patterning their lives after.

Phil V. Lewis serves as the Dean of the College of Professional Studies and Professor of Business at Oklahoma Christian University. He holds the BS from Abilene Christian University, the MA from the University of Denver and an EdD from the University of Houston.

---

48. Ibid.

Talents and Technology

Timothy DeClue and Jeff Kimball

As you examine the preponderance of technology on our culture and on the world of modern commerce, consider the parable of the talents found in Matthew 25.

> Again, it will be like a man going on a journey, who called his servants and entrusted his property to them. To one he gave five talents of money, to another two talents, and to another one talent, each according to his ability. Then he went on his journey. The man who had received the five talents went at once and put his money to work and gained five more. So also, the one with the two talents gained two more. But the man who had received the one talent went off, dug a hole in the ground and hid his master's money. After a long time the master of those servants returned and settled accounts with them. The man who had received the five talents brought the other five. "Master," he said, "you entrusted me with five talents. See, I have gained five more." His master replied, "Well done, good and faithful servant! You have been faithful with a few things; I will put you in charge of many things. Come and share your master's happiness!" The man with the two talents also came. "Master," he said, "you entrusted me with two talents; see, I have gained two more." His master replied, "Well done, good and faithful servant! You have been faithful with a few things; I will put you in charge of many things. Come and share your master's happiness!" Then the man who had received the one talent came."Master," he said, "I knew that you are a hard man, harvesting where you have not sown and gathering where you have not scattered seed. So I was afraid and went out and hid your talent in the ground. See, here is what belongs to you." His master replied, "You wicked, lazy servant! So you knew that I harvest where I have not sown and gather where I have not scattered seed? Well then, you should have put my money on deposit with the bankers, so that when I returned I would have received it back with interest. Take the talent from him and give it to the one who has the ten talents. For everyone who has will be given more and he will have

an abundance. Whoever does not have, even what he has will be taken from him. And throw that worthless servant outside, into the darkness, where there will be weeping and gnashing of teeth." (Matt. 25:14–30 NIV)

Ubiquitous computing. Digital convergence. Virtual reality. Even the words seem a bit frightening. The uncertain feeling they spark in most of us is not a welcome one. "Give me the *comfortable*," our hearts whisper to us, "the familiar, and the same world I knew yesterday—certainly not a world of unknown terms and technology, some of which appears to border on magic." This new world of technology is not the world we are prepared to live in. It is an unsettling place, a place we do not like to be. We feel a little bit like the third servant in the parable of the talents who was given a single talent to manage. Like us, he fears the horrible result that could happen if he misuses the precious talent provided by his master. Opting for the safest and least risky option, he buries the talent in a hole, hoping this action will protect his talent from the uncertainty of the unknown.

To his credit, he succeeds in achieving the goal he seeks. Yet, when the master returns, he is clearly dissatisfied with this servant. Again our hearts whisper a disconcerting word to us. "*Why?*" Didn't this servant return the talent in the same shape he was given it? Is that not good enough? The short answer is no. A more detailed answer reveals the truth that believers in Christ have the responsibility, indeed the privilege, of working for the glory of God and the benefit of His people. The answer provides some tremendous insight into why many believe it is a biblical principle to embrace and use computing technology, even cutting-edge technology that challenges many of the very assumptions we have about the physical world in which we live.

Technology—The Accelerator

Clearly, one of the principles the parable of the talents teaches us is that we are to take what we have and improve upon it. Technology provides the ability to accomplish the same amount of work as in the past, but to do so more quickly. Calculations that took days, weeks, or even years in the past can now be accomplished in a matter of a few thousandths of a second (a millisecond). Admiral Murray Grace Hopper, the designer of the COBOL programming language, was known for carrying a small bundle of eleven-inch long copper wire to her speaking engagements and then handing a few pieces out when she spoke. Her point was that light can travel only this eleven-inch distance in one-billionth of a second (a nanosecond) and that computer technology routinely operates in this realm of speeds. The fact that man could have created a machine that is able to accurately and routinely operate at these speeds in incredible.

In the early 1900s, as the Federal Government was faced with collecting census data, a disconcerting discovery was brought to the attention of the officials. Given the amount of time it took to collect, count, and record the data at the rate possible by hand, the census was in danger of not being completed until the next census ten years later was ready to be started again. Herman Hollerith stepped to the forefront with a new technology that could speed up this process—the hole-punched card—and saved the day. The ability to accomplish the same amount of work in less time is related to the parable of the talents. The two good servants would easily embrace this approach to work. It is the third servant—the one who buried his talent—who would be satisfied with the same work in the same amount of time.

Technology—The Amplifier

In the parable of the talents, the two servants who satisfied their master gave back more than they had been given; they had found a way to take their starting talents, and then multiply that gift – sort of like a worn-out water boy who is given a larger bucket so fewer trips are needed. Technology provides such an opportunity as well. On a trip to Washington, D.C., a tourist saw the Library of Congress for the first time. As the tour group entered one of the main rooms, the guide asked those in the group to look at the thousands upon thousands of volumes stored there. In a feeling of complete amazement, the tourist gazed upon the largest gathering of books he had ever seen in his life. The shelves packed with books seemed to extend row upon row and bookcase upon bookcase for as far as the eye could see. Then tour guide reported the group was only looking at books with titles beginning alphabetically A through F!

What tremendous difficulties we had at that time storing and effectively using large amounts of paper-based data. Today, storage technology has increased our ability to store such huge amounts of data that the contents of the Library of Congress (which amazed the tourist) can now be stored on a few DVDs (Digital Video Disk). Hard drives have increased their storage capacity from a few megabytes (millions of bytes) in the early 1980s to the terabyte (trillion bytes). It is more telling when we recall that each byte is roughly the equivalent of a single character. That is a lot of data!

Of even greater importance than our ability to simply store information is the ability technology gives us to search and interrelate the information we have stored. Once the storage devices were available to store such huge amounts of data, of course they were used—resulting in incredibly large repositories of stored information. These repositories are known—due to their ability to house the data—as *data warehouses*. *Data mining,* the techniques available for sifting through a data warehouse looking for unsuspected relationships between the data, have provided some interesting observations. Have you ever wondered why you will sometimes find cough syrup and bananas shelved in adjacent shelves in a Wal-Mart store? Wal-Mart Information Systems Division data miners discovered that many people who purchase bananas also purchase cough syrup at the same time. Placing the items nearer to one another is a strategic move with the goal of increasing sales. More important discoveries related to health, medicine and business have also been discovered using these techniques.

Technology—The Communicator

Someday, when we look back upon the era in which we now live, perhaps the greatest contribution of technology to the human experience will be the explosion of communication media. How different our lives are today in comparison to the world of a few short years ago! Seemingly, time and distance are no longer barriers to communicating with family and friends scattered across the globe. Perhaps Mother's Day is fast approaching and mother lives across the country. A card sent in the mail will not reach her in time. No problem. Send her an e-card. Simply go online, make a selection from the various formats available, compose a personal message and with the click of a button, mother gets the e-card the very same day.

Do you need to close a deal on some real estate but have to travel for business the same day? No problem. Your realtor can fax the document for you to sign and return in the same manner in which it was sent. Are you worried about missing an important phone call? Why? Cell phones now make it possible to be in constant contact with family or work associates at any time of the day and virtually anywhere in the world. Do you want to attend college and get an advanced degree but discover the college of your choice is too far away? No problem there either. Many colleges and universities and even some public schools are engaged in distance learning, where individual students can participate in lessons via the Internet or interactive televised lectures. Course work can completed from the comforts of home. Real-time chat. Instant messaging. Text messaging. Video conferencing.

All of these communication methods allow us to conduct business and stay in touch with family and friends without regard to time or distance.

Technology—The Problem Solver

Why do we have technology in the first place? Why are things always changing? Why is there always some new gadget, some new fandangled gizmo out in the stores? The simple answer is that technology is used to improve our situation in life. We want to get more things done. We want to have more information at our disposal. We want to communicate better. And we want all of that whenever it is convenient. There are obstacles to each of these worthy goals, and technology has helped us overcome them.

Consider the act of writing and sending a document to someone. For virtually hundreds of years, an important document would be written by hand and carried by messenger to its intended party. Of course, faster modes of transportation like the train and the automobile were invented to quicken the delivery service. The creation of the typewriter allowed document creation to be done quickly and in a much more readable format. Word processing software and printers allowed for better editing of documents, doing away with messy correction fluid. Documents could be printed, scanned and sent via fax over phone lines for quick delivery to their recipients. Now, documents can be quickly written and sent without ever being reproduced on paper, thanks to the ability to send items as email attachments or send data via the fax/modem in the computer. Creative use of technology makes all of that possible.

Software itself is nothing more than an attempt to "computerize" a process that is already being performed. The goal in mind is not to emulate but improve upon that process by making data easier to store and retrieve. Reports can be made in less time because software can analyze data and spot trends. Graphs can be added to a report with just a few clicks of a mouse button instead of painstakingly drawing such graphs by hand with a ruler and some markers. Research in schools. Advancements in medical diagnoses and treatments. Faster and safer transportation. Communication without regard to time or distance. All of this and much, much more is possible through the use of technology. And it is possible because the human mind is able to conceive of new and creative uses for technology, a powerful tool to be used in the improvement of existing circumstances.

Technology—The Creative Force

The Bible tells us we are created in God's image, an astounding statement on its face. Does this mean we achieve God's perfection and have complete understanding? Are we omnipresent and omniscient? Of course not. What then can God mean when He says we are like him? The most fundamental way we are like God is in our desire to be creative—to make something where there once was nothing—and we use the materials we are given. In times past, master craftsmen created amazing works of art like daVinci's Mona Lisa and Beethoven's Fifth Symphony and architectural marvels like the Eiffel Tower and the Empire State Building. Today mankind's greatest achievement is arguably the technological advances of our day.

Technological gadgets do not simply happen. They are the products of an analytical and creative mind, a mind that seeks knowledge and ways to connect what is known in new and exciting ways. The mind of man, formed by God, seeks to understand the world around him and even seeks to know more about God. This mind, which functions on many levels still not completely understood by even the most learned of doctors and researchers, is the most complex computer ever created, designed with purpose and careful planning by the Lord of all creation. It is this same mind that is fully capable of seeing the possibilities for good in the use of technology, to improve himself and his circumstances. Used wisely, it can ultimately bring glory to God.

Improve himself? Improve his circumstances? Bring glory to God? Weren't these the goals of the first two servants in the parable in Matthew, with respect to the talents provided to them by their master? Indeed. And these were the same goals that were not met by the servant with the one talent. The power of the mind crafted and designed by Almighty God, with its creative and analytical components working together, is a wonderful gift. It is this gift that lies behind the technology we see around us every day. Sure, there are wonderful things in the world today, amazing advancements and powerful tools used to accomplish tremendous things. But none of this would be remotely possible without the craftsmanship of God at work in us in the first place.

Timothy DeClue is Chair and Professor of Computer and Information Sciences at Southwest Baptist University. He holds the BS from Northwest Missouri State University and the MS and PhD from Southern Illinois University.

Jeffrey Kimball is an Instructor of Computer and Information Sciences at Southwest Baptist University. He holds the BS from Southwest Baptist University and the MS from the University of Central Missouri.

God's Mandate and Entrepreneurship

T. David Gordon and Jeffrey M. Herbener

WHAT HATH Jerusalem to do with Wall Street or Silicon Valley? Why should the Christian tradition consider entrepreneurship to be anything other than a tolerable insignificance (at best) or an intolerable expression of greed (at worst)? Why would a religion that proclaims a life beyond this one concern itself with the creative use of the present life? Is the idea of *Christian entrepreneurship* an oxymoron, equivalent to *Christian gambling* or *Christian prostitution*? Is entrepreneurship merely a means of fulfilling such vices as greed, covetousness, or envy?

While every legitimate human endeavor *can* be marred by human sin, this does not mean such endeavors are sinful *per se*. A musician could produce music as an expression of his rebellion against God, but this would not cause us to consider music *per se* to be an illegitimate activity. Similarly, parents could rear their children to fulfill their own frustrated goals and place inappropriate pressure on their children to achieve such; but this would not de-legitimate parenthood *per se*. In the same manner, we will argue that entrepreneurship is a legitimate human activity, indeed an activity that is *necessary* to the race's fulfillment of its created purpose. While not every individual need be an entrepreneur (any more than every individual need be a musician), every individual must recognize the necessity of entrepreneurship to humanity's achievement of humanity's created purpose. To establish this, the following will describe briefly the basic Creation Mandate (sometimes also called the Cultural Mandate), and then demonstrate the necessity of entrepreneurship to the fulfillment of that purpose and, therefore, some of the guiding principles that would inform a genuinely biblical approach to entrepreneurship.

The Creation Mandate

The Holy Scriptures record two great mandates that occupy the attention of the Christian community: The Creation Mandate and the Redemption Mandate. The Creation Mandate describes the nature and created purpose of the human; and the Gospel Mandate describes the role of the Christian Church in declaring how God reconciles a rebellious humanity to himself. In some quarters of Christendom, especially those American quarters associated historically with Revivalism, the Redemption Mandate has virtually eclipsed the Creation Mandate. In such circles, the creative energies of Christian people are almost exclusively channeled into the areas of what is often called "full-time Christian service." Sometimes in such circles, all other human activity is considered to be somewhat second-rate or insignificant.

It is not our purpose here to engage in a debate with the Revivalist tradition, but merely to assert that the broader Christian community has had a different opinion, with which I happen to agree. Historic Protestantism self-consciously objected to such a value distinction between holy and secular vocations, asserting instead an aggressive commitment to the Creation Mandate, and its corollary notion that all legitimate human labor can become an act of religious service. Indeed, Rome itself has come to embrace a very similar view, as expressed in Pope John Paul II's encyclical *On Human Labor*. In both the historic Protestant view and the Roman Catholic view articulated by Pope John Paul II, human rebellion has rendered our original creational mandate more difficult to fulfill, but it has not removed it from God's purpose. And similarly, both historic Protestantism and the Pope's view remind us that redemption itself is a restoration of humans to their original created relation to God and his original created purpose.

God's Dual Purpose in Creating Humankind—Cultivating God's Cosmos/Garden and God's Image

The first book of the Bible expends most of its time discussing the pre-history of Israel. Genesis chapters 12 through 50 record the calling of Abram, the promises made to him, and the initial fulfillment and reiteration of these promises through his descendants Isaac, Jacob, and Joseph. Prior to this, however, in the first eleven chapters of Genesis, Moses records thoughts about humanity in general, prior to the calling of Abram as a special individual through whose descendants God would rescue rebellious humanity. Thus, in this book that records Israel's pre-history, her pre-history itself is grounded in the pre-history of humanity *per se*.[49]

---

49. The book of Genesis is not without its interpretive difficulties, to put it mildly. It is neither my intention to entertain those questions here, nor to suggest (by not doing so) that those questions are unimportant. Genesis 1–3 frames the theological background to

In the first three chapters of Genesis, there is a record of the purpose of God in creating humans, and a record of their rebellion against this created purpose. The importance of these chapters is difficult to overestimate, since the remainder of the biblical account records how God rescues rebellious humanity, and restores it to its original created purpose. Thus, what we commonly call "redemption" is itself articulated biblically as a restoration of the original created order and purpose. Therefore, the entire Bible, from Genesis 4 until its conclusion in Revelation 22, harkens back again and again, explicitly sometimes and implicitly other times, to the narrative of creation and fall recorded in the first three chapters of Genesis.[50]

In the first two chapters, God's original created purpose for the human race is placed before us both explicitly and implicitly. Explicitly, the first two chapters describe the human's responsibility to cultivate the created order; implicitly, these chapters describe the human's responsibility to cultivate the human itself, as bearer of God's image. We will examine each of these in turn.

Cultivating God's Cosmos/Garden

Genesis 1 and 2 explicitly record God's mandate for the human race beginning with the first chapter of Genesis: "Then God said, "Let Us make man in Our image, according to Our likeness; let them have dominion over the fish of the sea, over the birds of the air, and over the cattle, over all the earth and over every creeping thing that creeps on the earth" (Gen. 1:26 NKJV). And then culminating in the establishment of the Garden

---

the Hebrew and Christian Bibles. They frame the Jewish/Christian conception of human nature and purpose, and inform all subsequent reflection in those traditions about the same. I refer to these chapters as a member of the Christian tradition and as a participant in that Jewish-Christian heritage that finds this explanation of human nature and purpose to be both satisfying and true. I do not speak as the definitive voice in solving all of the questions raised in these chapters.

50. Space does not permit, obviously, a full accounting of this. However, one cannot but note such overt realities as the fact that Paul the apostle refers to Christ as both the "last Adam" (1 Cor. 15:45) and the "second man" in contrast to the "first man" (1 Cor. 15:47); that he refers to Adam as a "type" of the coming Christ (Rom. 5:14); that he calls Christ the "image of God" (Col. 1:15), and refers to the redeemed as those who have been "created in Christ Jesus for good works" (Eph. 2:10), or those who have been "created after the likeness of God" (Eph. 4:24). In these and many similar texts, we note the unmistakably "Adamic" nature of New Testament theology. For just one exposition of this matter, one might consult Herman N. Ridderbos, *Paul: An Outline of His Theology*, especially chapter two, "Fundamental Structures."

and God's placement of man there in Genesis 2:15, the LORD God took the man and put him in the Garden to work it and keep it.

One might plausibly argue that two distinct mandates are recorded here: one regarding the created order itself and the other regarding the garden. Strictly speaking, there is an element of truth to such an observation, because the narrative does record the garden as a distinct place. However, it is also evident that the garden is (merely) an ideal microcosm of the cosmos itself; a place within the created order where its vast potential is more richly and exuberantly manifest. Adam is placed here (rather than on barren tundra or in a raft in the sea) because in microcosm the garden reflects the greatest, most-concentrated form of the created potential of the earth itself. This is reflected in a number of lexical similarities between the cosmos-mandate of Genesis 1 and the garden-mandate of Genesis 2 (such as references to "every living creature," "all livestock and to the birds of the heavens and to every beast of the field"). Therefore, for our purposes, it is sufficient to describe these two as essentially one: a mandate to cultivate the created order (Gen. 1:26–27), reiterated when the human is placed into a particular manifestation of that created order (Gen. 2:5–15).

Exercising Dominion and "Tending" the Garden

Genesis 1:26–27 explicitly records the created purpose of humanity as that of having "dominion over" all the earth, and over all the living things on the earth. Note also that it is humanity in its plurality that is considered: male and female. The human, as bearer of God's likeness/image, is the particular creature to whom the rest of the created order is entrusted. Its potential is to be discovered and cultivated; its beauty and usefulness explored, harnessed, and harvested in a responsible manner. Genesis 2 reiterates this mandate in a special place, the Garden of Eden, where the potential of the created order appears in an especially pregnant fashion. Twice in this narrative (verses 5 and 15), humans are described as having the responsibility to "tend," "cultivate," or "keep" the garden. And what will they cultivate? What specific potentials reside in this bountiful garden? The text describes this potential by two figures of speech, saying that the garden was "pleasant to the sight and good for food" (Gen. 2:9 NIV).

Of course, each of these figures is a metonymy for a larger reality, because the garden is not merely pleasant "to the sight" but to the ear, the nose, the palate, and the finger; it is pleasant to all of the senses. Similarly, it is not only good/useful "for food," but also for shelter, for clothing, and many other necessities. Put abstractly, one could say that the garden is both beautiful and practical, both lovely and life-sustaining, both pleasing and nourishing. Everything necessary either to enrich or sustain human life is latent in the garden, and the human race is given the duty of discovering and developing these two twin properties. The human, if faithful and responsible, will become both artist and artisan, creating (like God, in whose image he is made) what is delightful and what is useful. Genesis 2, therefore, brings greater detail to the more general mandate of Genesis one (exercise dominion). The dominion the human exercises is not the purposeless or destructive dominion of a demon, but the purposeful, creative dominion of an artist or artisan. The artist creates what is pleasing in itself; the artisan what is useful for a particular purpose; and humans will become both (though particular humans may be more efficient in the one task than in the other).

Cultivating God's Cosmos/Garden

Genesis one and two explicitly record God's mandate for the human race. "Let us make man" is parallel to "So God created man." Note that twice in each verse (four times total) we find that the human (in the plurality of "male and female") is described as "our image," "our likeness," "in his own image," "in the image of God." The human, male and female, is four times described as being in the image or likeness of God; and distinguished from the remainder of the creation by this designation. Not surprisingly, then, the Genesis narrative effectively describes God as being "over" all that he has made, and the image of God as being "over" everything else in the created order. Implicit in this four-times-repeated designation in this context is the reality that the creature invested with God's image is uniquely capable of exercising productive stewardship over the created order. While the created order itself has its own potential to be developed, the cultivation of the divine image will be necessary in order to develop that potential. Thus, while the mandate to cultivate the cosmos-garden is *ex*plicit in the narrative, the mandate to cultivate the divine image is *im*plicit.

Wherein does the image of God reside? What is it that distinguishes the human from other creatures as God's image? The history of reflection on this question has not produced complete consensus. Some suggest that "image of God" means nothing more specifically than sufficient correspondence to God to permit communication between Creator and creature. Others believe the matter is more specific and consists of a group of traits and abilities that distinguish the human from other creatures. And of course, more recently, the Western tradition (influenced by Darwinism) has demonstrated significant hesitation to describe the human as being different from other creatures, other than in degree. Even if *image of God* means something like a sufficient correspondence to permit communication, this would still imply some specific attributes. In what follows, then, are those traits or faculties that humans, as bearers of the divine image, have (at least latently) in a manner that other creatures do not: Humans have the following traits that God has and that other beings do not: rationality, imagination, wisdom, creativity, gregariousness, language, personality, self-transcendence, and moral, religious and aesthetic sensibility.

Regarding the human's creation in the image of God also suggests that the human would do some of the things God does. That is, if the Bible ended at Genesis 1:27, and we asked what we know about God, in whose image humans are made, the answer would be that God is a maker: He creates. He also manages his creation, in part by appointing humans to exercise dominion. Thus, a fully developed biblical understanding of the mandate to imitate God would suggest that the human imitates God's deeds as well as his traits. God makes, sustains, and redeems/repairs (commonly called creation, providence, and redemption); and the human made like him would imitate him by making, by sustaining and nurturing what is made, and by repairing that which is broken, damaged, or wounded.

An Extrinsic and Intrinsic Mandate to Cultivate

Taken together, the explicit mandate to cultivate the cosmos/garden and the implicit mandate to cultivate the divine image may also be thought of as a two-pronged mandate to cultivate both extrinsically and intrinsically: Humans cultivate what is outside and what is inside. Outside of ourselves, we cultivate the created order around us, discovering and developing that which is beautiful and useful; inside of ourselves, we cultivate those traits that reflect the divine image, because it pleases God to see Himself reflected in us, and because the cultivation of those traits is necessary to cultivating the properties of the created order.

The Dual Mandate Refused—Human Rebellion and the Curse

Sadly, the first two chapters of Genesis are followed by the third, in which there is a candid record of human rebellion against the creation mandate. The human, responsible for exercising dominion over "the creeping things" in obedience to God, disregards God's counsel and adopts the counsel of the serpent, inverting his creational responsibility and invoking God's just judgment. This judgment consists in mortality, in banishment from God's presence in the profoundly fruitful garden and in the curse placed upon the human indicating that his future labor will be different than his previous labor.

Now, human activity takes place in the midst of estrangement from God, estrangement from and friction with other humans (reflected in the statement to the woman: "Your desire shall be for your husband, and he will rule over you," (Gen. 3:16 NASB), and even frustration with the created order itself: "cursed is the ground because of you; in toil you will eat of it all the days of your life; both thorns and thistles it shall grow for you," (Gen. 3:17–18 NASB). There is a promise of redemption from this situation, cryptically embedded in the curse against the serpent: "I will put enmity between you and the woman, and between your seed and her seed; he shall bruise you on the head, and you shall bruise him on the heel" (Gen. 3: 15 NASB). Nonetheless, many generations will take place before this warfare, and humans will suffer under the curse for many, many years. Because of this rebellion and curse, the human's creational mandate is profoundly more difficult to fulfill; and yet even more urgent, because the once lovely and bountiful created order is significantly less beautiful and less nourishing.

Human Action

To achieve His twofold purpose of the creation mandate, cultivation of the His image in humans and cultivation of the created order, God made persons to act. He endowed them with the faculties necessary for human action, volition, purposefulness, intellect, foresight, imagination, creativity, and labor, and placed them in an orderly creation in which human action can occur. Humans share these traits with God and, therefore, when they exercise them they imitate God and not the beasts. Although endowed by God with godlike traits, human beings are finite and, therefore, their actions differ from His. Neither God nor beast, humans were made by God to engage in human action. Human action employs means to attain ends. The purpose of an action is to attain the end aimed at. Because he is finite, a human person cannot attain his ends immediately by a direct act of his will. He must employ means. In doing so, he must choose to strive toward the attainment of an end that he deems more urgent while simultaneously setting aside the pursuit of another end that he deems less urgent. Lacking innate knowledge of the order of creation, he must, also, discover that certain things in the created order have a particular causal connection to the attainment of his end and, therefore, can be used as means in action.

Having appertained that particular things are means in particular actions, he must, then, appropriate and employ them according to the design of action he deems effective to attempt to attain his end. In other words, God made each person in such a way that his action presupposes controlling the use of, or one might say having personal ownership of, means.

Entrepreneurship

Finitude also implies that a person cannot be certain his action will succeed. The decision to act does not instantly realize the end aimed at. Time elapses as action proceeds and time implies change, not all of which can be perfectly anticipated by a finite being, one who lacks perfect knowledge of all the cause and effect relationships in the created order. Entrepreneurship refers to that element of human nature that determines the degree to which action either succeeds or fails in attaining its end. All the other faculties involved in action, volition, purposefulness, intellect, imagination, creativity, and labor come to naught without entrepreneurship. The essence of entrepreneurship is the foresight that harmonizes the decision to act in the present with the realization of the end in the future. Foresight is a person's ability to envision a future state of affairs that can be brought about by his action. It involves being able to apprehend the potential of the created order to attain human ends, a potential that remains latent until action under the guide of entrepreneurship realizes it.

While God comprehends perfectly all of the cause and effect relationships that govern the created order, humans do not. They must, instead, discover them in an ongoing learning process. Every discovery of the workings of nature, every invention and innovation that puts these discoveries to work brings humans closer to knowing the mind of God and, thereby, improves their ability to achieve the purpose God gave them. God made the beasts to endlessly repeat their instinctual patterns of behavior, but humans He endowed with reason and imagination so that they could act creatively to realize more fully the potential of the created order. Humans reduce themselves to beasts if they refuse to exercise the traits they share with God to realize the potential in God's created order (and themselves), and instead merely repeat primitive, traditional methods of production. To discover new uses for resources and methods of production, to create new capital goods and enterprises, in short, to exercise entrepreneurship is essential to obeying the creation mandate.

As God is supreme in action, so He is in entrepreneurship. His perfect foresight implies that what He wills to attain, He attains perfectly. When

He created the universe, He made no mistakes. He declared the creation good because it turned out exactly as He envisioned it. Even the reconciliation of sinful humans to Himself, He planned before the foundation of the world and accomplished perfectly in the death and resurrection of His Son. Unlike that of God, man's foresight of the future is imperfect. Because his entrepreneurship lacks perfection, a human person can err and fail to attain his end in action or fail to attain it fully. He can, therefore, experience regret from the wasted opportunity to have acted beneficially.

Creation Mandate and Entrepreneurship

Entrepreneurship is that special aspect of commerce that addresses new possibilities for productive human activity, and/or for the sharing of the benefits of such. *American Heritage* defines the entrepreneur as "a person who organizes, operates, and assumes the risk for a business venture." This definition will work perfectly adequately, and the first two traits rightly counter-balance the common tendency to think of the entrepreneur merely as a risk-taker, speculator, or even gambler. The entrepreneur is more than a venture capitalist (who also plays a legitimate role in commerce); at the heart of theistic entrepreneurship is the creative organizational activity that characterizes the entrepreneur: the entrepreneur has a vision for a new way of exercising responsible stewardship over the created order.

That vision will ordinarily express itself in one of the following five ways: a new service to humans, a new use of natural or human resources; a new means of harvesting or producing resources, a more efficient service or use of resources, or more humane labor environment. When the modern hospital was first conceived, it intended to provide a new service—specialized and standardized health care that could not be affordably achieved in homes. Later, when hospices began, they offered a new service the hospital had not offered—a humane management of terminal illnesses in the more-comfortable, more-supportive environment of the home. When natural gas (and later, electricity) was harvested (and domesticated), heat and light could be provided in a manner necessary to the further development of urban societies. When Henry Bessemer developed a new process for producing iron, he effectively employed combustion and forced air to produce what we now call steel, and developed from the natural order a material that was both superior to, and profoundly less expensive than, other construction materials and methods. Improved lighting and ventilation enhanced the physical characteristics of the labor environment; some firms have provided on-campus day-care and dining facilities to ameliorate the separation of the laborer from the family. Good managerial entrepreneurship has discovered ways of making labor both more efficient and, in some cases, more humane. In these and many other ways, the entrepreneurial spirit has conceived new means of employing natural or human resources for the mutual good of the human race. Any entrepreneurial vision that achieves any of these goals is praiseworthy, and those who assume the risk of attempting such progress are properly rewarded for their efforts, just as those who labor in other ways are rewarded for theirs.

Theistically, the goal of entrepreneurship is not merely profit; all lawful labor is profitable. Entrepreneurship is that particular labor that is eager to discover new ways of harvesting the bounty of the created order for the good of its inhabitants, to discover the manifold wisdom of God in the work of his hands. Thus conceived, entrepreneurship is one of the profoundest of vocations, a vocation that permits one to love both the Creator God and one's neighbor simultaneously.

T. David Gordon serves as Professor of Religion and Greek at Grove City College. He earned his BLA at Roanoke College, his MAR and ThM at Westminster Theological Seminary and the PhD at Union Theological Seminary.

Jeffrey M. Herbener is Chair and Professor of Economics at Grove City College and a Senior Fellow at the Ludwig von Mises Institute. He holds the BS from Nebraska Wesleyan University, and the MS and PhD from Oklahoma State University.

10

Competition, Success, and Ethics

> "Render service with a good attitude,
> as to the Lord and not to men."
> —Eph. 6:7

> "Therefore do not be anxious about tomorrow,
> for tomorrow will be anxious for itself.
> Sufficient for the day is its own trouble."
> —Matt. 6:34 ESV

> "Train up a child in the way he should go;
> even when he is old he will not depart from it."
> —Prov. 22:6 ESV

> "I can do everything through Him who gives me strength."
> —Phil. 4:13 NIV

> "Periodical godliness is perpetual hypocrisy."
> —Charles Spurgeon

> "Only he who believes is obedient; only he who is obedient believes."
> —Dietrich Bonheoffer

> "The only thing necessary for the triumph of evil
> is for good men to do nothing."
> —Edmund Burke
> (commonly credited)

"I believe God made me for a purpose, but he also made me fast, and when I run, I feel God's pleasure."
—Olympic runner Eric Liddell in the film Chariots of Fire

"Worry does not empty tomorrow of its sorrow; it empties today of its strength."
—Corrie ten Boom

"If you are going to be a champion, you must be willing to pay a greater price."
—Bud Wilkinson

"I will let no man control me by making me hate him."
—Booker T. Washington

"Only one life, 'twill soon be past—only what's done for Christ will last."
—Anonymous

"Success is the maximum utilization of the ability that you have."
—Zig Ziglar

"The ultimate measure of a man is not where he stands in moments of comfort, but where he stands at times of challenge and controversy."
—Martin Luther King, Jr.

Perspectives on Competition

Sharon G. Johnson and Galen Smith

Competition is so engrained in business literature that we tend to take it for granted. We assume that everyone knows what we mean by competition, and that while competition does raise some concerns (particularly in the way competition is carried out), in many business classrooms competition is assumed to be the best approach to handling most business transactions. Additionally, many teachers use competitive processes in their classrooms. Grades are often awarded on a student's competitive standing on class points/averages. Some courses utilize business simulation games where teams of students compete either with "the game" or with each other for market success.

Our search led us across a great many definitions of competition. We offer four different definitions. We discovered that part of the complexity (and contentiousness) of the discussion surrounding competition is that it is defined in so many different ways between various fields of study (for instance, economics versus psychology), and between authors in the same field.

> For our purposes, competition will be defined as a process through which success is measured by directly comparing the achievements of those who are performing the same physical activity under standardized conditions and rules.[1]

> In thinking about competition it is important to define it in as neutral a way as possible . . . Competition is a perfectly general human phenomenon which results from scarcity. It is because the prizes to be won are limited and the resources to be allocated are finite that competition exists. Competition is simply a way of resolving conflicts of interest in society. It may take many forms: it may be a game of sport, or it may be the violence of the jungle, it

---

1. Coakley, Jay J., "Competition in Sport—Does It Prepare People for Life?" In *Sport in Society: Issues and Controversies*. 3rd Ed. Times Mirror/Mosby College Publishing, St. Louis, 1986, 206.

could be a beauty contest, an essay prize, or a job interview. As the examples indicate, the basis of competition may be skill, beauty, violence, or just chance.[2]

The economists' concept of competition is very specific. A competitive market is one in which there exists substantial freedom of entry and exit for products and people. A competitive car market is one in which new firms are free to enter and compete or in which old firms can leave the business. By contrast a non-competitive market would be one [for example] in which existing producers set prices by agreement among themselves and kept out potential competition . . . Sometimes competition may be an end in itself as in a game of sport. But in the economic sphere the purpose of competition is to provide goods and services to the consumer as cheaply as possible . . . In economic life competition is not an end in itself but a means to an end.[3]

Competition arises whenever men strive for identical objects which cannot be possessed in common. Indeed, the act of such striving is the very essence of competition. . . . (1) *Deliberate competition* is an act of striving with other people in order to (a) do something better, (b) be thought more of, (c) obtain more power, [and/or to] (d) possess more material wealth than those other people. . . . (2) *Involuntary Competition* is the act of striving for identical objects which cannot be possessed or enjoyed in common, but striving solely for the sake of the object and not with reference, conscious or unconscious, to the other people concerned.[4]

Our review of definitions has left us believing there is a very real phenomenon called competition, but it is too big to be captured in its whole by any one definition from any one discipline or author. What we can do is to offer an initial set of observations that focus on what most of the definitions have in common (themes in concert), and then a set of contrasts that capture the differences creating tensions among the definitions (themes in conflict). As already demonstrated in this paper's examination of both definitions and differences, there is no single "accepted definition or perspective on competition. As we shifted our study toward integrating what we had so far learned about competition, we assumed, correctly, that there would be conflicting points of view.

2. Griffiths, 6–7.
3. Griffiths, 71–72.
4. Harvey, 8, 10, and 18–19.

Our studies revealed that some Christians have concluded that Christianity and competition are essentially incompatible, while others claim that competition is not only compatible with Christianity but also that Christianity actually enhances one's competitive performance. We will review some of the literature speaking to these differences, but the diagram and discussions following that initial review propose a framework for understanding the tensions between various perspectives in the Christian community about the problems with and prospects for competition within that community of believers.[5] Our research leads us to posit that there are two key dimensions Christian face when confronting competition. The first dimension focuses on the way a Christian chooses to relate to competition: at the extremes Christians can choose to fully engage in competition, or to be fully disengaged (estranged) from competition. The second dimension focuses on the reaction Christians can have to competition: at the extremes they can challenge competition (for example, question its necessity or desirability, debate its ends and/or means), or accept and co-exist with competition (as it currently manifests itself in whatever setting the Christian finds themselves). The result of the relational and reaction dimensions is four positions which seem to capture at least the boundary marks of Christian perspectives on competition.

Christ Resists Competition

The essential tenet of this perspective is that competitive desires and Christlikeness are inherently, irreconcilably opposed. The belief is that the Bible condemns competition as an evil condition to be mourned (and in the life of the Believer, to be removed). Christians are seen as in "combat" with the evil effects of competition. The existence of competition is viewed as a testimony to man's fall from God's kingdom. Our role as Christians is to remain separate from the competition because Christians involved in competition will experience corruption of their loyalties to God. This perspective would say that those Christians who advocate competition are doing so only as a pretense to sanctify their desire for worldly pleasure and success. The thrust of the teaching of scripture is how to avoid the entrapping lure and attendant perils of competition.

5. The framework for the diagram and table that follows is our original work but owes its structure to Richard Niebuhr's work in *Christ and Culture* (Harper Torchbooks, NY, 1951) and an article titled "Christ and Business: a Typology for Christian Business Ethics," (published first in the Journal of Business Ethics, Vol. 8, 1989, 883–885) by Louke van Wensveen Siker. Neibuhr developed four possible relationships of Christians to culture and Siker applied this framework to the business environment.

Christ and Competition in Partnership

The essential tenet of this perspective is that the Bible commends competition as an exciting condition to be enjoyed. The claim is that Christianity and competition are not only compatible but inclusively complementary—that is, Christians both can and should compete, and doing so helps us grow spiritually, physically, socially, and economically. Competition is a present to be enjoyed and cultivated wherever possible and in that competition we can truly experience God's delight. Christ comes to competition as encourager, and the existence of competition in our world is perceived as testimony to God's common grace for His kingdom resulting in aspirations for excellence that help in both personal and community growth and development. Christians involved in competition will experience confirmation of their loyalties to God. Successful (principled) competition is seen as a reward and blessing from God. Scripture helps us to apply God's principles to competition. In this view there is no inherent conflict between Christianity and competition—rather, they are seen as mutually supporting each other.

Christ Reforms Competition

In this perspective Christ comes to competition as transformer, seeking to rediscover God's design for competition. In this view many of the practices of competition *in the world* (such as cheating, a win-at-any-cost mentality, seeking to exploit others) are to be challenged. The aim is to seek the reformation of competition, not its elimination. Our role as Christians is to engage in competition and seek to make a difference in both the means and ends of competition. Christians involved in competition will experience covenanting of their loyalties to God as they seek to bring God's power and purposes into competitive arenas and as they target competition as a process to be exploited for God's glory. Scripture offers a variety of insights of how to use God's power in competition to advance His kingdom. Whether on the racetrack or in the marketplace, Christians are called to engage as God's warriors to reclaim competition for His glory.

Christ and Competition in Paradox

This perspective focuses on the very real tensions Christians can experience in competitive situations. This perspective on competition is best summarized as one of irreducible complexity. Our role as Christians in this view is to engage in the paradoxical call to be *in*, but not *of*, competition—that is, participating in competition where we are called (and gifted?), yet fully knowing that competitive situations may bring conflict in our lives as the demands of the *game* may raise issues about our loyalties to God in non-easily resolvable ways. The Bible, in this perspective, does not specifically embrace competition nor does it condemn it outright. There is a recognition, however, that the Bible's overall "position" on competition is one that repeatedly cautions about competition. Indeed competition is seen as an uneasy condition to be subordinated to God's priorities and principles. Christians are reminded, in this perspective that our real aim is to witness for Christ. To the degree that competition provides a platform for our witness, it may prove to be helpful in advancing that *missionary* cause. The table that follows offers a series of contrasts designed to explore in more detail the specific points of difference between the positions.[6]

Summary of Four Generic Christian Perspectives on Competition

	Christ resists competition	Christ and competition in partnership	Christ reforms competition	Christ and competition in paradox
Christ comes to competition as . . .	Judge	Encourager	Transformer (redeemer)	Shepherd
The Bible . . .	condemns competition	commends competition	controls competition	cautions about competition
The Biblical perspective on competition is best summarized as . . .	Combat	Compatibility	Challenge	Complexity
Competition is seen as . . .	an evil condition to be mourned	an exciting condition to be enjoyed	an existing condition to be redeemed	an uneasy condition to be subordinated

6. Intentionally these positions are painted in the extreme. Any given Christian might actually hold "parts" of each of the positions in theory and/or in practice. Further, someone who might identify themselves as essentially in agreement with any one of the positions as a whole might be in disagreement with any one of the parts of the positions as described here.

Competition results from . . .	God's judgment	God's delight	God's design	God's grace
Competitive desire and Christ-likeness are . . .	inherently opposed	inclusively complementary	intendedly necessary	independently parallel
The existence of competition is a testimony to . . .	man's fall from God's kingdom	God's common grace for His kingdom	the realization of God's kingdom on earth	God's special grace for His kingdom people
Our role as Christians is to . . .	remain separate from the competition	get involved in the competition	make a difference in the competition	be in, but not of, competition
Christians involved in competition will experience . . .	corruption of their loyalties to God	Confirmation of their loyalties to God	covenanting of their loyalties to God	conflict in their loyalties to God
The claim that someone is called to engage in competition . . .	is a pretense (to sanctify one's desire for worldliness)	is a present (to be enjoyed and cultivated wherever possible)	is a position (to be exploited for God's glory)	is a possibility (depending on one's ends and means)
God's Word tells those in competition	how to avoid the perils of competition	how to avoid the perils of competition	how to use God's power in competition	how to achieve God's purposes in competition

Some Conclusions

There is no common agreement in the Christian community about either the definition or the value of competition. While there are those whose praise of the value of competition seems unabashed, many more seem to feel a tension about both the means and ends of competition. A great deal of the discussion of competition in the Christian community seems anecdotal rather than analytical. This is especially true in the arena of sports competition. A variety of popular books have been written by Christian athletes who rather uncritically note how competition has made them more reliant on God, more conscious of the need for teamwork, and more humble (as they cope with losses and injuries). While all this may be true, such discussions hardly provide the thorough empirical and theological examination that competition should invoke.

It is common in some Christian circles to point to Paul's use of competitive sports metaphors as a biblical endorsement of such competition. It is our conclusion that such use of scriptural analogies is simply wrong. For example, because Paul discusses "running the race" in several of his letters does not mean he endorsed foot racing. An analogy is a comparison of Phenomena A to Phenomena B in order to clarify our understanding of Phenomena A. If I say that "life is like gambling" I am not, thereby, automatically endorsing gambling. Our examination of some Christian defenses of competition leads us to conclude that too often those defenses are based on faulty exegesis of scripture. Because this study is still exploratory, we are continuing to examine the perspectives on competition present in different Christian traditions. Our initial impression is that the fundamentalist, evangelical Christian tradition has been more likely to embrace the *Christ and competition in partnership* perspective while the Quaker/Mennonite tradition has embraced the *Christ resists competition*.

We are quite aware that within the Christian community some see competition as praiseworthy while others see it as pathology. It is our intuitive (at this time) assertion that a full, exegetically correct analysis of scripture regarding the themes of competition and cooperation will reveal a decided scriptural bias for cooperation. Further, we would also assert that competition is seen in scripture primarily in a negative way. We suspect that an honest evaluation of competition from a biblical perspective would, at the very least, lead us to be far more cautious about the untempered endorsement of competition we have seen among many evangelical Christians today. At the most, we believe a study of scripture freed from pre-agenda to seek endorsement for competition might lead us to some very radically different conclusions.

Sharon G. Johnson serves as the Director of Institutional Research, the Director of Graduate Programs, and as Professor of Management at Cedarville University. He holds the BS, MBA and DBA from Florida State University.

Galen Smith is Professor of Economics at Cedarville University. He has a BBA from Washburn University, an MS from Kansas State University, the MDiv from Grace Theological Seminary, and a DMin from Trinity International University.

Defining Success

Rodger W. Minatra

"For I know the plans I have for you"—[this is] the Lord's declaration—"Plans for [your] welfare, not for disaster, to give you a future and a hope" (Jer. 29:11). When our children were young, our family liked to watch a television series called *A-Team*. Colonel John "Hannibal" Smith, played by George Peppard, and the A-Team pulled off some of the most incredible military operations imaginable, and though his plans almost never unfolded just he planned, they always worked out in the end. One of my favorite parts in the show was when Hannibal Smith, cigar clinched between his teeth, would say, "I love it when a plan comes together."

In the TV series, Hannibal Smith's plans were consistently successful because success was written into the script. Those in charge of the show worked it all out so that the bad guys were defeated and the good guys—the A-Team—ended another mission victorious. In real life, George Peppard didn't follow the same script as his fictional character Hannibal Smith. An alcoholic for almost thirty years and multiple bad marriages, many considered him to be almost self destructive. Friends and fans felt that he never really found the success that he deserved. In the end Peppard died of pneumonia, a result of a lifetime of smoking and weakness from chemotherapy sessions for treatment of his cancer.

Some of us have experienced some of the same highs and lows that George Peppard experienced. All of us have experienced difficulties, hardships, and failures to some degree. Life can be tough; jobs go sour, relationships become rocky, finances fall flat, and good plans turn into failures. In such times we can find ourselves doubting our ability to ever achieve what we set out to accomplish; we wonder if we will ever be successful. However, as Christians we can take heart, even in the midst of difficulties, hardships, and failures. Like the fictional character, Hannibal Smith, the script writer of our lives has a plan for our success. Plans may not always work out like we scripted them, but according to God's word, they will work out. "We know that all things work together for the good of those who love God: those who are called according to His purpose" (Rom. 8:28).

People have different definitions of success; but when measuring success, most people use four general categories: wealth, position (including fame and power), knowledge, and pleasure. God's word addresses each of these and warns us that none of them bring lasting or true success. King Solomon, in Proverbs, warns us against the constant pursuit of wealth and tells us that it is a fleeting type of success with no guarantee for happiness. Examples of this reality are found throughout history. Some of the richest people in the world die lonely and depressed, unable to find the lasting happiness they hoped their fortune would provide or purchase. "Don't wear yourself out to get rich; stop giving your attention to it. As soon as your eyes fly to it, it disappears, for it makes wings for itself and flies like an eagle to the sky" (Prov. 23:4–5).

Jesus spoke of the success that accompanies position when he addressed the mother of James and John after her request that her two sons be allowed key leadership positions in his kingdom—one to His right and the other to His left. "But Jesus called them over and said, 'You know that the rulers of the Gentiles dominate them, and the men of high position exercise power over them. It must not be like that among you. On the contrary, whoever wants to become great among you must be your servant, and whoever wants to be first among you must be your slave: just as the Son of Man did not come to be served, but to serve, and to give his life—a ransom for many'" (Matt. 20:25–28). The Apostle Paul addressed the success of acquiring knowledge in 1 Corinthians 8:1. He says that knowledge without humility, leads to intellectual vanity. King Solomon addressed both the pursuit of knowledge and pleasure. He said that the pursuit of pleasure accomplishes nothing, and much study makes the body weary (Eccl. 2:2; 12:12–13).

Fortunately, God has a different view of success—one that includes an eternal prospective. God's design for our real success is not to make us wealthy and it is not to give us positions of power or fame. His definition of our success is not for the self gratification of knowledge and not for our own pleasure. Rather, God's divine goal for us—His design for our success—is to make us like His Son, Jesus. God works all things together so that we might grow in our Christlikeness and be glorified with Him in eternity.

Knowing how God defines success provides direction and priority in our own planning process. It also adds a sense of security and joy to our lives, knowing that God is interested in our success. Though knowing God's definition of success does not free us from the responsibilities that we have as stewards of His provisions, knowing how He defines success does provide us a biblical worldview of success. God's definition of success gives us the freedom and incentive to invest our lives in something that neither moth nor rust can destroy.

One of the greatest benefits of knowing how God measures success is realizing that our success is not based on our own abilities and determination. God not only has a plan for our lives, but He has a desire to see that plan through to completion. "I am sure of this, that He who started a good work in you will carry it on to completion until the day of Christ Jesus" (Phil. 1:6). The script God has written for our life includes a successful ending. With that perspective, it is safe to say, even before our own story is completed, "I love it when a plan comes together."

Rodger W. Minatra is an Associate Professor of Business Administration at Southwest Baptist University. He holds a BS from Arizona State University, an MA from the University of Denver and the EdD from the University of North Texas.

Success: The Never-Ending Journey

David B. Whitlock

A NEWSPAPER reporter was interviewing an old rancher who had experienced a good deal of success in his ranching operation. The reporter asked the man to what he would attribute his success. With a twinkle in his eye the man said, "It's been about fifty percent luck, fifty percent weather, and the rest is brains."[7]

What is success anyway, and what makes a success? It depends on who you ask. And there are plenty of people to ask. A Google search on the internet reveals 926 entries under the subject of success, and that doesn't include all the related links. One could surf the internet for quite some time trying to discover all there is to know about success. Then there are all the books on success. Most bookstores will include entire sections on success, sometimes mingled into the *self-help* section. An entire lifetime could be spent simply studying about success before ever getting around to being one!

So, what exactly is a success? Again, it depends on who you ask. Winston Churchill defined it as consisting of "going from failure to failure without loss of enthusiasm."[8] Reverend Tope Popoola says true success "is not necessarily about being the best at all cost. It's about DOING your best at all times. If you do that long enough, who knows, you might just end up being the best."[9] Author Christopher Morley says "there is only one success—to spend your life in your own way."[10] Somewhat similarly, Jack Canfield, co-creator of the Chicken Soup for the Soul Series, and author of *The Success Principles: How to Get from Where You Are to Where You Want to Be*, says success is to be defined individually. "You might want to win a Pulitzer Prize, another person might want an Olympic gold medal, someone else might want to just live out in the woods and not be bothered and paint.

---

7. Michael Hodgin, ed., *1001 Humorous Illustrations*, (Platteville, Co. : Saratoga Press, 1992), 227.

8. http://www.secretsofsuccess.com/article/quotes.

9. http://insightoftheday.com/quotetext (accessed 10/12/06).

10. http://brainyquote.com/quotes/author.

Success is being able to do what you want to do and go where you want to go and be what you want to be and have what you want to have." [11]

Success would include portions of all those definitions. Most motivational speakers and coaches, along with leadership and self-help authors will have their definition of success. But what about God? How does God view success? Does He define it? Is success even a topic we should venture to inquire of in regard to God? Since the Bible does refer to the subject of *success*,[12] it is not only permissible but most appropriate that we ask the God of the Bible about this subject. What is the biblical view of success and how should this impact our lives? That is the subject we will investigate. God is immensely interested in us, and therefore our successes and failures concern him. What we must keep in mind is his perspective of what we are when we are successful. Once we have a clear vision of what it means, from a biblical perspective, to be a success, we can move in that direction. The Bible should be our source since it is there that God has revealed the truth about Himself.

First Things First

Back in 1986 Tony Campola wrote a book entitled, *Who Switched the Price Tags?*[13] Campola suggested that the world is like a store which some mischievous youths have broken into at night and switched all the price tags. The next morning, the value of the merchandise is confused. The analogy to life is that the things we so often deem as valuable in reality are not, and that which seems of little worth really is. We must therefore change our thinking about what is important and what is not.

The same lesson applies to success. We must drop notions of what success is or isn't, according to the world's way of thinking. Too often, by a secular standard, success is evaluated primarily by quantitative measures. "How much money do you make? How many times did you win? How much power does your position give you?" This is not to say these are never factors in measuring some degree of success. It is to say they are not the only or primary ways we evaluate or define it, at least according to the

11. *Keys to success Decide what you want, take action, persist*, Interview by Mary A. Jacobs, Knight Ridder Newspapers, cited in http://www.dailyitem.com (accesses 5/06/05).

12. *The New Living Translation* Complete Concordance cites 48 entries under the words "success," "successful," and "successfully." See John R. Kohlenberger III and James A. Swanson, eds., *New Living Translation Complete Concordance* (Wheaton, Illinois: Tyndale House Publishers, Inc.), 1003.

13. Anthony Campola, *Who Switched the Price Tags?* (Copyright Anthony Campola, all rights reserved, 1986).

Bible. So, what indicators do we find in the Bible that give us an idea of how God views success?

In the Gospel of Mark, a man came to Jesus. He was a man of learning, a man of biblical scholarship. Mark describes him as a "teacher of the law." Apparently this man had some understanding of what Jesus was about, for after his conversation Jesus told him, "You are not far from the kingdom of God" (Mark 12:34 NLT). The man had a question. He was in effect asking, "What is the most important commandment? Of all the commandments, which one should I focus on to achieve approval in God's sight?" It seems he was asking what it takes to be a success in God's eyes. So, take note. What would Jesus say?

You know the answer. Jesus told him there were two commandments: "The most important commandment is this: 'Listen, O Israel! The Lord our God is the one and only Lord. And you must love the Lord your God with all your heart, all your soul, all your mind, and all your strength'" (Mark 12:29–30 NLT). Jesus went on to include the second: "The second is equally important: 'Love your neighbor as yourself.' No other commandment is greater that these" (Mark 12:31 NLT).

This religious leader saves us miles of investigation in discovering just what the biblical notion of success is. There we have it: true success is loving God with all we are and as a consequence, loving others as ourselves. The first question of success would then be, "How's your love life with God?" And the follow-up would be something like, "And how well are you loving others?" Jesus tends to derail our natural tendencies to define and measure success in terms of possessions, prestige, or power.

In another place Jesus said something similar. "Seek first the Kingdom of God and His righteousness and all these other things will be added unto you" (Matt. 6:33 NKJV). Again, the spiritual life is paramount; a life lived loving God and embracing his Kingdom as we love others is the primary indicator of a successful life because that which is eternal is life. In other words, we are not primarily physical beings who happen to accomplish a measure of spiritual success along the way to the more important earthly goals. We are rather primarily spiritual beings whose pursuit of eternal things may attract, along the way, lesser symbols of success such as money, power, and status. The main goal is to know and love God.

It would appear we would be safe in saying, based upon these Scriptures, that according to the view of Jesus, a success would be anyone who loves the Lord, and remember Jesus identified himself as one with God, with all their being as they seek the Kingdom of God. In that seeking, they will love others. It seems to come down to loving God and whoever happens to be closest to us at any given moment. Success then is a relationship of loving God and as a consequence of loving Him, loving others in a web of relationships where we love as God would have us love.

Immediately our priorities are set because we know our purpose. We were made to love God, and as a result we love others. The relationships we form as we love create a Kingdom-of-God-like quality to life. Success is not something we do apart from God, our families, or friends. Success is loving God and others. They become part of the success formula: God and others are our priorities and loving them becomes the measure of success. Success is not primarily about how much we have or own or know (even about the Bible). It's about how we are loving God and others as we seek his Kingdom.

Oswald Chambers said it like this: "We will set up success in Christian work as the aim; the aim is to manifest the glory of God in human life, to love the life hid with Christ in God in human conditions." He concluded that, "Our human relationships are the actual conditions in which the ideal life of God is to be exhibited."[14] We live our life to love God. The better we know him, the better we are able to love. Making a decision to love him and others is the beginning of the journey toward success.

A Vision is Worth a Thousand Words

If we could visualize what it is to love God with all we are and others as ourselves, we would be seeing the Kingdom of God. Jesus told us to pray for this Kingdom to come soon (Matt. 6:10) and for his will to be done on earth as it is in heaven (Matt. 6:11). We have already seen that His will for us is to realize our purpose in being created to love him. Only then will we find fulfillment in life; only then will we experience true success.

In the Kingdom everything is turned upside down: the first are last and the last first; we are to give rather than receive; we are to do to others as we would like them to do to us. It's not the world we find on Wall Street. That's why it is essential that we receive a vision for living the Kingdom within the world where we are. As we love God with all we are, we are given assignments in expressing that love to others. Those assignments are usually based on a combination of our gifts and the needs around us. As we are sensitive to God's voice, He gives us a vision. Loving God and others is not something that takes place in a vacuum. It is implemented in the real world around us.

14. Oswald Chambers, *My Utmost for His Highest* (News York: Dodd, Mead, and Co., 1935), 321.

God gives a vision for what He wants. He gives us a vision for the kind of person He wants us to be. He gives us a vision for our ministry to our family and friends, and beyond that, others whom we don't even know. It's that vision that propels the believer into expressing the Good News of God's love to others. We must get still before God so that He can begin to burn within our souls the vision he wants. The implementation of this vision becomes an expression of the love we have for God. The more we love God, the more likely we are to succeed in fleshing out that love to others in our world. Faith then becomes a requirement for the fulfillment of the vision.

In the book of Acts, Luke tells us that Paul received a vision. He saw a man from Macedonia pleading with him to come to Macedonia in northern Greece and help them. So, Paul acted on that vision. He stepped out in faith. The result was that the gospel was opened to Europe. The word traveled west to Europe rather that east to Asia. What a difference a vision makes. It's worth more than a thousand words!

William Carey opened India to Christian missions in 1792. Because of his tremendous work for God at a crucial time in Christian history, he is known as the Father of Modern Missions. Carey's vision for missions was born in part at least by reading of all books, *The Last Voyage of Captain Cook*. In that book Captain Cook had speculated about the likelihood of missions to the east and noted how unlikely it would be. Carey longed to prove his statement wrong. He began to study the possibilities. He made notes and hung a homemade map on his wall. He even stitched a globe out of leather. His sister-in-law said of William, "More than once I saw him stand motionless for an hour or more in his garden, absorbed in his tense thoughts and prayers till his neighbors judged him beside himself."[15]

Where will our vision come from and what will it be? That depends on many factors, including the needs around us, our natural inclinations, and spiritual gifts. It is essential that we listen to God; it is unlikely that we will be all that God wants us to be and do what he wants us to do for him if we are unwilling to receive a vision that declares who we are to be and how we are to minister to our families, friends, and others . We shouldn't be surprised that as we become absorbed in that vision, our neighbors and friends, like William Carey's, judge us to be just a bit "beside ourselves."

---

15. S. Pearce Carey, *William Carey* (London; Hodder and Stoughton, 1926), 51.

PART II: A MATTER OF WORLDVIEW

Bringing it Down

Dave Thomas, the founder of Wendy's fast food restaurants said that success begins within, on the inside. He believed that unless a person's attitudes and beliefs were right, real success would never be achieved in the world.[16] We have discussed how belief gives rise to vision. As we love the Lord with all our heart, mind, soul, and strength, and our neighbors as ourselves, we pray for a vision. The vision is a picture, of sorts, of how our assignment looks in Kingdom relationships. The inner aspect, as Thomas notes, has to be right, or the outer relationships will be all wrong. Success may be achieved in terms of the world's view, but not by God's standards. The question then becomes, how do we bring the vision into reality?

Prayer and a seeking of God's will are constants in bringing the vision into reality. God gave Nehemiah a vision to rebuild the wall around Jerusalem. The walls around the city of God were down, and Nehemiah was convicted. God called him to lead the people in rebuilding those walls. Nehemiah prayed. God gave a vision. Implementing it was a step by step process. It involved careful planning, team building, and problem solving. Nehemiah demonstrated courage, integrity, and perseverance in bringing the vision into reality.

Is it appropriate to ask for success? As long as we recognize that success is being who God wants us to be and doing what he wants us to do, why not? As we humbly seek to love God, is it wrong to ask him to enable us to do that? Certainly not. That is especially so when we realize that on our own it is impossible to love God and others as we are commanded. But we are reminded that "What is impossible for people is possible with God" (Luke 18:27 NLT).

Recognizing our human frailties, we call on God to lead us to successful ministries. What is a successful ministry? It is living the love of God as best we can. We ask God to lead us to minister in such a way that he approves what we do for him. Thus, Moses asks God to "satisfy us each morning with your unfailing love" (Ps. 90:14 NLT). He prayed that God's work would be seen among his people so that the Lord would "show us his approval and make our efforts successful" (Ps. 90:17 NLT). And when Eleizer, Abraham's servant, goes on what he believes is a mission expressing his love and loyalty for his master, he begins his journey to find a wife for Isaac by praying, "Please give me success today, and show unfailing love to my master, Abraham" (Gen. 24:12 NLT).

---

16. Jack and Garry Kinder, *21st Positioning, Proven Selling Precepts* (Dallas: Taylor Publishing Co., 1996), 120.

Competition, Success, and Ethics

The stronger we believe something, the more likely we are to bring it into reality. Unfortunately, our natural tendency is toward the negative. Left to our undisciplined selves, we will think negatively about ourselves and even God's willingness to do something positive (successful) with our lives. Much of our inner dialogue is negative. Prayer changes all that. We get in touch with the God of all possibilities, and he changes our thoughts.

The Scriptures admonish us to "let God transform you into a new person by changing the way you think" (Rom. 12:1 NLT). Paul goes on to say this change in our way of thinking involves an honest evaluation of who we are. We are God's children, given the assignment of communicating Christ's work of reconciliation to the world. Our thoughts are therefore positive in the sense that we can through Christ accomplish the task or assignment He has given us.

Paul said it like this: "I can do everything through Christ who gives me strength" (Phil. 4:13 NLT). Paul had his priorities right. He was focused on the task God had given him. Because it was from God, he believed God would give him the strength to accomplish it. Why is Paul considered such a successful missionary? Because he had an unswerving belief in what God wanted him to be and do, and he believed that what God had assigned, He would provide the means to accomplish.

To the degree that we believe it, it will happen, when our belief is grounded in God's vision for us. That's when success begins to be noticed. It was there, within the mind, as it was with Nehemiah or Paul. As the strength of that belief leads to action, success is recognized. Success then is simply becoming who God has called us to be, and doing what God has called us to do. We live the dream. It becomes reality.

Along the way we are of course met with obstacles. This serves to test the resolve of our belief. When Henry Ford came up with the idea for a new engine, the V-8, he had his men draw up plans and give it to the engineers. The engineers studied the plans and kindly but firmly told Ford it couldn't be done. Ford said, "Produce it anyway." Again they told Ford it was impossible. Again Ford said, "Produce it anyway." For some six months they struggled. They couldn't figure out a way to make it work. But Ford insisted they find a way. They labored another six months. Nothing. At the end of a year, they still said it couldn't be done. Ford wouldn't accept that. Finally they discovered a way to build the V-8 engine.[17] Ford's belief was much, much stronger than that of the engineers. He was not only a man of vision; he firmly believed in the possibility of his vision becoming

---

17. John Maxwell, *Developing the Leader Within You*, (Nashville: Thomas Nelson Publishers, 1993), 142.

a reality. Had he allowed negative self-talk to dominate his thinking, it is most unlikely Ford would have persisted like he did. It takes strength of character to bring a vision into reality.

Follow Through

I played at golf for a brief period of time. One thing I was told to do when I swung the club was not just to hit the ball but to follow through. I don't completely understand it, but the follow through made the golf swing more effective. When I was a college student, I sold cemetery property door-to-door during the summers. My sales manager would tell me, "The fortune is in the follow-up." What he meant was that following through on the sales call would not only solidify the sales but lead to other customers as well. He was right.

Following through is also essential in responding to God's desire for us in His Kingdom work. It can mean the difference between failure and success. The reason following through is so essential is because it is so easy to quit. It's been said that the road to success is dotted with many tempting parking places. In the Book of Numbers, the Israelites, under the leadership of Moses, were in their first approach to the Promised Land. This was before the twelve spies were sent in and the people began their wilderness journey. In Numbers 10, the people are approaching the Promised Land but are complaining. Moses' scout then refuses to go forward and threatens to return to his home and family. Moses is challenged on every side. Yet in the midst of it all, we read these words: "They moved on each day" (Num. 10:34 NLT).

So much of success is moving on each day. Call it follow through or persistence or what you will, it simply means not giving up on the plan God has planted in your heart. Numbers 10 closes with Moses shouting in triumph! He was not to the Promised Land. In fact, he would never get there. Yet he was successful in being the man God called him to be and doing what God called him to do. This is true despite his personal failures.

It's the failures, more often than not, that keep us from getting there. We focus on our mistakes. Sometimes they are a result of our own doing; other times someone or something beyond our control caused them. Affixing the blame doesn't really help. Most often, the only thing to do is "move on each day." That's following through. Success rarely comes to those who stand still. Eric Allenbaugh has said the common way of spelling success is "p-e-r-s-i-s-t-e-n-c-e." He points out the example of the cleaning product *409*. Can you guess where the name came from? The researchers had 408 "unsuccessful" attempts before the final product was developed. The name for the product is a testimony to the power of persistence![18]

In the movie *Chariots of Fire*, Harold Abrahams, the British track star, loses a 100 meter heat. For a long time afterward he sits in the stands. He is motionless as he stares down at the track. The only words he can muster are to tell of his pain in being beaten by a fraction of a second. His future wife tries to console him, but Abrahams turns to her and says, "If I can't win, I won't run."

She wisely responds, "If you don't run, you can't win." Her words sting him back to the reality of the race ahead, and Abrahams went on to win the finals.

It's easy, isn't it, to stay in the stands and brood? Success comes when we get out of the stands and get back in the race. Paul said it like this: "Don't you realize that in a race everyone runs, but only one person gets the prize? So run to win!"(1 Cor. 9:24 NLT). And lest we forget, Paul goes on to remind us that the prize is an eternal one. Therefore we "run with purpose in every step" (1 Cor. 10:26 NLT). If our purpose is to please God by loving Him with all we are, then temporary setbacks only refine our love. We won't win a race we refuse to run; success is not giving up on God's ability to use us.

Are we there Yet?

John Maxwell has rightly emphasized that success is not a destination but a journey.[19] We are never *there*. We never, at least on this side of eternity, completely arrive. Actress and writer Carrie Fisher has said, "There is no point at which you can say, 'Well, I'm successful now. I might as well take a nap.'"[20] We are ever in the process. The key is keeping our eyes on the heavenly vision. As we read through that roll call of God's faithful ones in Hebrews 11, we repeatedly read the phrase, "It was by faith . . . " It was by faith that these saints fulfilled what God assigned them to be and do. It certainly wasn't easy or it wouldn't have required faith. The chapter concludes with these words: "All these people earned a good reputation because of their faith, yet none of them received all that God had promised. God had something better in mind for us, so that they would not reach

---

18. Eric Allenbaugh, *Wake-Up Calls* (Austin: Discovery Publications, 1992), 111.

19. John Maxwell, *The Success Journey* (Nashville: Thomas Nelson Publishers, 1997). Maxell says, "Success is a journey," 1.

20. http://www.briantracyinternational.com (accessed at newsletter@briantracyinternational.com, March 16, 2006).

perfection without us" (Heb. 11:39–40 NLT). As faithful as they were, even they never fully arrived.

Here's something else to notice about that passage. Their journey is part of our journey as well. Those who are listed in this chapter of the Bible, which is referred to as "faith's hall of fame," never completely arrived until the death and resurrection of Christ. Christ is the focus of our success journey. We are not traveling alone. We walk a united front with other believers. Part of our success anticipates the fulfillment of God's plan with others.

What God has in mind for us is Christ. The writer of Hebrews begins Chapter 12 by underscoring the fact that the race we run is the one God has set before us. He is the one who called us to love Him and others. That can only happen in the miracle of faith that He initiates. As we stay the course on this success journey, we are successful by "keeping our eyes on Jesus, the champion who initiates and perfects our faith" (Heb. 12:2 NLT). That is our success journey. And it's a journey worth running.

I do not know the origin of one of my favorite stories. It tells for me much of the true meaning of success. It's the story about a young man who left his village in search of success. He sought to find his way in the world. As he traveled the journey, he came to a fork in the road. There by the road sat an old man, the wise man of the nearby village. "Tell me," the young man demanded, "which of these roads leads to success?" The wise man did not say a word. He only pointed down one of the roads. The young man eagerly walked in the direction the old man had indicated with his pointed finger. It seemed the young man had been gone only a very brief time when he returned bruised and wearied from the journey. "I must have misunderstood you," he said to the wise man. "I am seeking success."

Again the old man remained silent and only pointed the traveler in the same direction. So, again the young man set off on his journey and once again within a brief period of time, he returned. This time he was more battered, bruised, and fatigued than before. By now the young man had grown exasperated. "I asked the way to success, you foolish old man! Why, the road you sent me on is full of jagged rocks, steep hills, and treacherous cliffs. I think it is impossible to climb! What I asked for was the road to success."

The wise old man just sat there in silence. Slowly an understanding smile crossed his face. He said, "I know, son. I know. But success is that way. Yes, it's just beyond the jagged rocks, and steep hills, and treacherous byways. It is just beyond the bruises, the setbacks, and the pain."[21]

---

21 Adapted from *Bits and Pieces*, (March 2005), 16–17.

We are ever on the journey but never arriving completely. Our calling is to love the Lord and others. As we do, success is ultimately determined by our looking beyond ourselves to the heavenly vision on a road that has been secured for our safe arrival based on the promise of our Lord. And there we receive the prize of success: a welcome home from our Father.

David B. Whitlock is Pastor of Lebanon Baptist Church in Lebanon, Kentucky, and teaches in the School of Theology of Campbellsville University. He holds the BA from Baylor University, the MDiv from Southwestern Baptist Theological Seminary, the MTh from Princeton Theological Seminary and the Ph.D. from Southern Baptist Theological Seminary.

He Was a Successful Man

David Wesley Whitlock

ONE OF the most outstanding examples of a successful man is one of my own heroes, Joseph. Consider Joseph and how he handled the hard knocks of life found throughout his life. Despite setback after setback, Joseph is defined in the Word as a *successful man*.

Joseph's youth apparently was spent in relative ease. As Genesis 37 describes, Joseph was loved by his father Jacob above all of his older brothers. The son of Jacob's beloved Rachel, Joseph garnered the majority of his father's attention, interests, and affection. Jacob bestowed gifts upon Joseph, and at least one was a beautiful coat signifying Jacob's honor of Joseph. Such favoritism caused great jealousy among his brothers. So great was the animosity and jealousy that his brothers had for him that the Bible says that they could not even speak kindly to Joseph. They hated him and couldn't even speak peaceably with him. His dreams—his visions—exacerbated this hatred.

When he was seventeen years old, he had a pair of dreams. In the first, he dreamed that as he and his brothers were binding their sheaves in the field when suddenly his stood up and his brothers' sheaves began to bow down to his. In the second dream, he saw the sun and moon and eleven stars bow down before him. The dreams clearly communicated to the family that this young brash upstart would someday be exalted over his family. What a promise! Joseph may have wondered when this would occur, when he would be elevated. Would it be tomorrow, next month, next year?

What Joseph could not possibly have known at the time is that despite the reality that God would indeed exalt him in ways beyond his comprehension, Joseph first had to be prepared. What Joseph did not know in that simpler time of his life was that he was about to be enrolled in the *University of Hard Knocks,* and that several trials awaited him before the vision would come to pass. What Joseph came to understand was that God's timing is perfect, despite the appearance and circumstances, and that God would be working all things together in Joseph's life, in his brothers' lives, his father's life, and even in the affairs of the entire known world. All things were being worked together by God from the tiniest, seemingly insignificant event to major world events such as the politics of world governance, even the weather patterns that affected crop success and failure.

Before he completely understood what was happening, Joseph found himself in a situation that certainly seemed to defy his vision of God's promise. And so began his education, the hard knocks, the trials, and setbacks, and sufferings. Cast into a pit by his brothers and nearly killed by them out of their hatred, I believe I would have wondered whether or not I understood the promise: "This isn't going according to plans is it? This isn't the fulfillment of the promise, the vision, is it?" Yet Joseph seemed even then to exhibit some deep sense of God's providence. Never revealed to be a complainer or griper, Joseph seemed to keep his head held high with a calm peace that God was working all things together for good. Somehow in the pit, he seemed to grasp that God was going to work it all out.

As a band of heathen Midianites—Ishmaelites—passed nearby, his brothers sold him as a slave for twenty shekels of sliver. I wonder if those traders wondered why they took that particular route that particular day. What luck it was that they passed by just in time to find such a fine, strong slave out there! They didn't understand it was providential as they took him to Egypt and sold him into the house of Potipher, the captain of Pharaoh's guard. If I had been Joseph, I would have been tempted to wonder how in the world this could have been part of the vision to be exalted. It seems more like a series of humiliations instead. But Joseph seemed to have some grasp of providence, understanding that this too was all under God's sovereign control, despite appearances.

In Genesis 39, we catch a glimpse of why during these setbacks that we really never see Joseph questioning God, why we never really see Joseph becoming bitter or angry, though the temptation would have been great. Instead we see what kept him going, how he survived in the face of so many negatives. "The Lord was with Joseph and he was a successful man" (Gen. 39:2). His success was not dependent upon his station in life any more than ours is. It wasn't dependent upon his wealth or lack of it, or on how much he knew. His success (like ours ultimately will be) was dependent upon having the Lord with him. So it was that Joseph became a trusted servant and all of Potipher's affairs were put under his authority. Even in slavery, Joseph was successful. Even in slavery, the Lord was with Joseph. Even in slavery, Joseph seemed to understand that God was working all things together for good.

Then, just when things began to look up for Joseph, there were more bitter consequences. Potipher's wife attempted to seduce him, and when he refused to give in to her advances, she accused him of attempted rape. To save reputation, Potipher had Joseph cast into Pharaoh's dungeon. I must admit I would have been questioning God at this point: "God, did I understand you? Is this the plan? I did the right thing! This is my reward?" But Joseph was a better man than I, and the scripture states: "But the Lord was with Joseph and showed him mercy and He gave him favor in the sight of the keeper of the prison" (Gen. 39:21).

So much so, that the keeper of the prison (possibly even Potipher himself) put Joseph in charge of all others in prison. Even in prison under false accusations, even while he was punished as a result of doing the right thing, the Lord was with Joseph. Joseph, even in these circumstances, seemed to have a quiet understanding that God's providence would work it all together for good. He seemed to understand that no matter what the situation was, God was still on His throne and would use even these setbacks as part of His divine plan.

What was Joseph's secret? It was not power, not position, not connections and networks, not financial resources, not status. Joseph's success was found in the words: *the Lord was with him*. What a powerful statement. The Lord was with him and he was a successful man. God's definition of success is so radically different than the way our society believes. True success is found in knowing God, and in having the Lord with you. The most astounding fact in the world is that the Creator of all things condescended to us that we should know Him, and that He would be with us. Anything less than a relationship with the Creator must be defined as failure.

David Wesley Whitlock serves as the Associate Provost, Dean of the College of Business and Computer Science, and Professor of Business Administration at Southwest Baptist University. He earned his BS and MBA from Southeastern Oklahoma State University, and the PhD from the University of Oklahoma.

An Ethics Primer

Troy Bethards

INSIDER TRADING. Falsified audits. Inordinately high CEO salaries. Mismanagement of pension funds. From Enron and WorldCom to the local clothing store owner who secretly videotapes clients in the dressing room, business is often portrayed as corrupt and manipulated by dishonest and immoral individuals. Though there are many professionals who perform their responsibilities ethically and legally, the headlines reveal the sad truth that many in business are driven by baser instincts. When faced with ethical dilemmas, how should the believer respond? The following ethical frameworks should be understood by all professionals and those preparing for careers in business.

Theological Framework

The theological framework is important for Christians because believers recognize that they answer to a higher authority and seek God's guidance and direction in their lives. Making sure that their actions align with God's desire is greatly influences their decision making. Therefore, the primary question in ethical decision making is, "What is the desire of God?" To properly address this question, the theological system places its focus on the love for God and mankind, as well as respect for others.

Addressing the importance of love as a basis for determining morality, Hill references "ethicist Lewis Smedes [who] characterizes love as 'the hinge for every other moral rule to swing on.'"[22] The source for using the love for God and mankind is found in Matthew: "Jesus replied: 'Love the Lord your God with all of your heart and with all of your soul and with all your mind.' This is the first and greatest commandment. And the second is like it: 'Love your neighbor as yourself'" (Matt. 25:37–39 NIV).

Another aspect of the theological framework is respect. Respect for all mankind is reinforced in 1 Peter: "Show proper respect for everyone:

---

22. Hill, A. *Just Business: Christian Ethics for the Marketplace.* (Downers Grove, IL: Intervarsity Press 1997), 47.

Love the brotherhood of believers, fear God, honor the king" (1 Peter 2:17 NIV). If this framework were used to come to an appropriate conclusion, one must answer the question of whether a specific business action interferes or misdirects a person's love for God and His ways. One must also consider whether a particular action encroaches upon the command to love and respect others. If the action violates any of these positions, then it should be considered unethical. For Christians, the theological framework would be an important component in concluding whether a particular situation or action is acceptable.

Legal Framework

Carl Fulda indicates how legal requirements can be used as an ethical framework when he states, "The law reflects the thought prevailing in the community, including its moral values, and thus it becomes a basis of business ethics."[23] Therefore, it could be said that if enough people within a democratic society deemed a particular action unethical, then that society would establish laws preventing such action. This statement would indicate that everyone has an equal voice in the determination of such laws; however, that is usually not the case.[24] Special interest groups influence legal considerations, which may not be the desire of the majority in a society. Hosmer also points out that even advocates of the legal framework will indicate that this system establishes only minimal standards as moral judgments.[25] It seems evident that the legal framework has shortcomings. Even so, the rules of law may still be used as a guide in determining whether a particular action is appropriate and provide an indication of how society feels about a particular action.

Economic Framework

One of the components of capitalism, as set forth by Adam Smith, is the ability of individuals to better themselves. Individuals are rewarded under a capitalist system when they are better suited for certain positions, have special talents or have special information. One aspect of the capitalist system is captured by Shaw and Barry when they stated the following ideal that coincides in with Adam Smith's *Invisible Hand* doctrine: "We will, if

---

23. Stevens, E. *Business Ethics.* (New York, NY. Paulist Press 1979), 118.
24. Hosmer, L. T. *The Ethics of Management* (3rd ed.). (Irwin/McGraw-Hill 1996), 74.
25. Ibid., 62.

left free, engage in labor and exchange goods in a way that results in the greatest benefit to society."[26]

Utilitarianism Framework

Utilitarianism is focused on the outcome. The goal is to pursue the greatest positive result for the greatest number of people. The utilitarianism framework can be viewed from two different perspectives. Jeremy Bentham and John Stuart Mill are credited with developing utilitarianism or more specifically *act utilitarianism*. Act utilitarianism specifies "that we must ask ourselves what the consequences of a particular act in a particular situation will be for all of those affected."[27] If the action in a particular situation will bring greater benefit compared to another alternative, it should be pursued; if not, then this action is not acceptable.

A second utilitarian perspective is *rule utilitarianism*, which is offered by Richard Brandt. This version states that moral codes should be used to apply the standard of utilitarianism rather than individual actions.[28] The focus should be on the moral codes that are most appropriate for society, so that satisfaction or utility is increased. Thus, rule utilitarianism is used to help determine whether an action is appropriate in general and not just as it pertains to a particular situation.

Justice Framework

Justice is an important value in America's society and is one of the values on which this nation was founded, as represented by the last portion of the *Pledge of Allegiance* of the United States, which concludes "with liberty and justice for all." As Hosmer addresses John Rawls theory of *Distributive Justice*, he states that, "Justice is felt to be the first virtue of social institutions, as truth is the first virtue of systems of thought."[29] As a cornerstone in society, justice is utilized as a means to address ethical dilemmas.

There are three approaches one could take when utilizing justice in an ethical dilemma. The first type of justice is *Compensatory Justice*, which attempts to appropriately compensate an individual who has been *wronged* in some manner. The second classification is *Retributive Justice*, which at-

---

26. Shaw, W. H. and Barry, V. *Moral Issues on Business*, 5th ed. (Belmont, CA. Wadsworth, Inc. 1992), 157.

27. Ibid., 62.

28. Ibid., 78.

29. Hosmer, L. T. *The Ethics of Management*, 3rd ed. (Irwin/McGraw-Hill 1996), 95.

tempts to appropriate consequences to individuals who have engaged in an undesirable action. The final form of justice is *Distributive Justice*, which focuses on whether benefits and costs to society are distributed in a right, just or fair manner.

In Rawls' theory of Distributive Justice, cooperation of individuals is necessary for the promotion of society as a whole. The distribution of items that are of benefit can be handled in a number of ways. Benefits could be given in equal portion to each individual, according to a person's level of competence, according to what a person needs, how much an individual contributes or how much effort one expends.[30] Hosmer also points out that individuals will pursue a proper distribution of the benefits that society creates; and that this distribution of benefits will likely be unequal as long as it shows that the unequal system works to the benefit of everyone within a society.[31] Therefore, if it is determined, for example, that the distribution that results from insider trading is not just, or that cooperation between individuals is decreased, then the action is not acceptable. However, if trading with privileged information results in an appropriate distribution and increases cooperation between individuals, the action is ethical.

Many struggle with their call to a professional vocation. Business is often presented in unflattering light, especially as corporate scandals are plastered on newspaper headlines, the evening news, and nationally distributed magazines. But for the Christian, business can be a high and holy calling. Christian business professionals ought to approach their calling as sacred. When approached from the standpoint that business is about meeting the needs of others, one's career goals can take on a whole new perspective.

Business and free enterprise is compatible with biblical practices and expectations if approached with the view of providing housing, clothing, food, and products that improve the lives of its users. Innovation that improves the health, welfare, and provides needed goods and services for others, when done ethically and in accordance with biblical principles and expectations, is a noble calling. When approached from the standpoint of serving others, the practice of business becomes a worthy profession to pursue. Servant leadership and meeting the needs of others is indeed a calling that is consistent with a Christian worldview, if it is practiced according to the high standards set forth in God's Word.

Troy Bethards is an Assistant Professor at Southwest Baptist University. He holds the BS from Southwest Baptist University, the MBA from Missouri State University and the DBA from Anderson University.

30. Ibid., 96

31. Hosmer, L. T. (1996). The *Ethics of Management* (3rd ed.). Irwin/McGraw-Hill, p. 96.

Ethics and the Marketplace

Bart C. Craytor

It all begins with thought. Every action we take, every move we make, is borne of thought. The progeny of thought provides the basis for our conduct. Psychologist have examined, classified, and interpreted human conduct over the years. Philosophical pontificators promote profound postulations from such perceptions. Inspection of the intricate details of one's behaviors provides the examiner a glimpse into the soul of the observed. Whether we examine the actions of an individual or that of a social group or culture, we cascade back to the fundamental foundation that each such behavior begins with thought. Our earthly limitations prevent us from legislating thought, so accordingly we proscribe acceptable conduct and criminalize unacceptable behavior.

Dr. Howard Gardner, the Harvard psychologist who redefined intelligence in his publication, *Frames of Mind*, furthers his discourse in *Intelligence Reframed*. He discusses the need for an expansion of the members of the intellectual universe to include subsets of talents and characteristics traditionally outside of those tested on standardized intelligence exams. Dr. Gardner listed seven intelligences in his original publication. They are (1) linguistic, (2) logical-mathematical, (3) musical, (4) bodily-kinesthetic, (5) spatial, (6) interpersonal, and (7) intra-personal intelligences. In *Intelligence Reframed*, he considers three additional candidate intelligences: a natural intelligence, a spiritual intelligence, and an existential intelligence. Gardner supposes, "[I]f the abstract realm of mathematics constitutes a reasonable area of intelligence (and few would challenge that judgment), why not the abstract realm of the spiritual?"[32] Dr. Gardner does not purport that these are new characteristics or traits. His paradigm includes areas of discussion formerly ignored by others in his professional society.

With our attention directed to Gardner's defined intelligences, what is the effect of spiritual intelligence on our lives? How does this relate to our ethics? Ethics is a blend of social interaction and intra-personal

32. H. Gardner, *Intelligence Reframed*, pg 53, Basic Books.

reflection. It is a standard that varies by occupation and station in life, but establishes minimum criteria for those who enter the marketplace in that occupation or station. Most on this earth live within a societal concept of a governing body. Laws, edicts, regulations, rules, mandates, ordinances, orders, commands, and directives issued by the governing body through one or more of its instrumentalities or agents instruct, constrain or otherwise describe acceptable behavior within the context of its jurisdiction or reach. Typically, behavior outside of the described boundaries is unethical. The converse is not necessarily true. Obedience to the law does not equate with ethical behavior. Ethics has a higher calling. Not only does it demand compliance with the law, it requires steadfast observance of principled behavior beyond the law.

Professional ethical behavior is conduct within accepted principles established by peers. A professional's conduct is generally governed by the various codifications of ethical guidelines for each profession or occupation. Failure to comply with the established rules of conduct may result in the loss of the privilege to practice in the chosen profession. Yet the requirement of ethical behavior for long-term success in the marketplace pervades activities for which there is no licensure board or peer review. The marketplace will demand ethical considerations for a lasting presence. Capitalism despises those who have poor reputations for value or integrity. It is in these latent rules and precepts we find lurking the cannons of ethics, not as a trap for the weary, but as constant reminder that unacceptable action produces unacceptable results. Worthy actions produce worthy results and unworthy actions produce unworthy results[33]. The equation becomes a simplistic summary of desired behavior. In practice, we find the simplicity is remarkably absent and perhaps evasive.

As we review the text in this field guide, we find words committed to encouraging good behavior and establishing moral character. When we discuss truthfulness, are we dedicating our actions to the cause of the consumer/client/patient/employer or to the cause of the Christ? When we speak of integrity are we to undertake the philosophies and practices of our employers, or remain true to our core life values. Genesis declares: "the imagination of man's heart is evil from his youth" (Gen. 8:13 NKJV). Is it proper to transact with the unsaved on their level? Shall we subscribe

---

33. The "Deuteronomic Formula" (Deut. 4:40; 5:29, 32, 33; 28:1, 2). According to this philosophy, living right and practicing good will result in blessings of prosperity in this life. On the other hand, doing evil will reap only suffering and negative repercussions in this life (Deut. 28:15, 58–63). *The Women's Study Bible*, Thomas Nelson Publishers, Note to Ecclesiastes 8:10–17.

to the demands of the marketplace for the benefit of profit at the expense of our reputations or Christian characteristics? Should our Christian testimony suffer to complete the transaction? Is there a justification facilitating an unethical means to the ends? Or does the concept of ethical behavior proscribe integrating core principles into our daily practice? What are the benefits of demanding ethical conduct? The administrative agencies governing those practicing in licensed professions claim ethical guidelines preserve honor and integrity in the profession as a whole and protect the clientele served from injury or loss when they are particularly vulnerable to deception or trickery.

The sobering thought, however, is that violations of the rules of ethics are not to serve as the basis for any cause of action, but that the guidelines are to be utilized by the governing agency or board in disciplinary matters.[34] Most disciplinary proceedings are confidential to public knowledge and review and are even granted privilege from discovery in our courts. We recognize the shortcomings of our principles and guidelines and the difficulty in preventing unethical behavior. The childhood tales of Robin Hood illustrate our acceptance and elevation to hero status of clandestine citizens who commit crimes to right the wrongs of an oppressive Sheriff of Nottingham.[35] The doctrine of civil disobedience underscores our societal appreciation of breaking the law for a good cause. But what standard are we to adopt?

Those who serve in a licensed profession are required to subscribe to the rules of reason issued by the government. For others, continued existence in the marketplace will require ethical behavior. But for our eternities, the true defining principles of ethical behavior are found in the Bible. Principles not born of human minds but eternal in the heavens. God judges both our actions and our thoughts. We as fleshy creatures determine thoughts by permitted or accepted conduct and forbidden conduct, but God knows the very thought that engaged the action. When we join Jesus on the mountainside as He preaches, we observe examples of judgment upon thoughts. In the fifth chapter of the Book of Matthew, Jesus sat down and began teaching His followers. Jesus warns us that if we are merely angry at our brother we are in danger of the judgment for murder. In following verses we read: "Ye have heard that is was said by

---

34. Annotated Model Rules of Professional Conduct 3rd Ed. 1996, American Bar Association, Page xvii; Similar provisions exist in the Code of Ethical Conduct issued by the American Institute of Certified Public Accountants and the American Medical Association's Preamble to the Code of Ethics governing physicians.

35. Paul instructs us otherwise. In Romans 13:1–7, Peter reminds us to obey God first. Acts 5:29.

them of old time, Thou shalt not commit adultery. But I say unto you, that whosoever looketh on a woman to lust after her hath committed adultery with her already in his heart" (Matt. 22:27–28 KJV). We can feel the sting of judgment when we have yet to lift a finger.[36]

Ethics is putting into practice the rules of reason. Living by the rules. As Christians, we are challenged to act and think by the rules. An antiquated standard of conduct for attorneys indicated that they were to avoid the appearance of an impropriety. The goal was to protect the reputation of the profession as a whole at the cost of disqualifying oneself from accepting a new matter. However, the committees of the legal profession found that the standard was too difficult to define, and the rubric would forego any new client-lawyer relations where any anxiety (a thought) might surface. Thoughts are too pervasive, and an argument could be made in nearly any situation permitting one to find some appearance of an impropriety no matter how slight. Our biblical standard is much more rigid. We are compelled to comply with the laws, in action and in thought, while our "imaginations are evil from youth." We are to avoid any conduct finding reproach by our neighbor. Walk the Christian walk. Talk the Christian talk. Follow in the Lord's footsteps and imitate Christ (Heb. 13:7).

Justice demands meting out discipline in relation to the crime. Ethics require no more or no less than that which justice requires. The Old Testament provides that, "And he that killeth any man shall surely be put to death. And he that killeth a beast shall make it good; beast for beast. And if a man cause a blemish in his neighbour; as he hath done, so shall it be done to him; Breach for breach, eye for eye, tooth for tooth: as he hath caused a blemish in a man, so shall it be done to him *again*. And he that killeth a beast, he shall restore it: and he that killeth a man, he shall be put to death. Ye shall have one manner of law, as well for the stranger, as for one of your own country . . ." (Lev. 24:17–22 KJV). We know the wages of sin is death according to Romans 6:23. Sin regardless of the grade, misses the mark and requires judgment accordingly. Yet we have a merciful God as attested to in Jeremiah 3:12. Mercy is that act of withholding the punishment that justice requires. Mercy allows the redaction or abolition of punishment rather than fully executed justice. Finally, we have a gracious God as John 1:14 explains. Grace is a gift without consideration. Justice is what we deserve, mercy spares us from what we deserve, and

---

36. Justification for completion of the act can be made if one is going to suffer the consequences of the action for its mere contemplation. Completion of the act, however, has additional consequences such as facing the courts and administrative tribunals, (replacing the beast, an eye for an eye, etc.).

grace provides us what we don't deserve. Ethics is above and beyond that which mere law requires. Ethics establishes principles and guidelines of our thoughts thereby governing conduct of our lives. Grace provides us salvation when we miss the mark.

It is further interesting to note that ethics does not wait in the closet with the attorney's suit, the doctor's coat, the judge's robe or the store with the merchant's wares. Ethics govern our lives both inside and outside the marketplace. Ethics permeates our homes. These rules of reason are established to insure that those who choose these lofty professions are willing to commit themselves to high standards of conduct in every context. There are requirements of continuing education to maintain competence. What about exercise and fitness? Requirements to avoid substance abuse to maintain clear judgment and good health are promulgated. The public's confidence in an intoxicated surgeon is questionable at best. Our professions will not allow reliance upon one whom it presumes unreliable. Our marketplace might temporarily place trust in a new venture, however, if the rule and guide of actions is tainted, we are assured that failure is certain to follow. We reap what we sow as outlined in Galatians 6:7–8 and Psalm 1:1–6.

How do we score in our spiritual intelligence? Do we rank among the apostles or flounder with the Gentiles? Dr. Gardner indicates that the effects of a high spiritual intelligence occasionally produce a contagion: "People affected by a spiritual individual pass on a reflected spirituality to others. Indeed, many religions have spread by just such a charismatic process that circulates among, and is expanded by, disciples and disciples of disciples."[37] As we expand and grow in our ethical knowledge, we hope also to expand and grow in our areas of influence. As our realm of influence expands, so does the possibility of receiving criticism and examination of our motives and core values. Principled conduct becomes more mandatory and less of a choice. "There are a thousand hacking at the branches of evil to one who is striking at the root," exclaims Henry David Thoreau. Edmund Burke is commonly credited for saying, "All that is necessary for the triumph of evil is that good people do nothing." Ethical considerations would require action in such circumstances, not toward the branches but extraction of root [thought].

Christian ethics mirrors the marketplace in that it requires an integrated approach to our lives and not merely our occupations. Christian ethics delineates our rules and guides of thought which precede our actions. Christian ethics establishes disciplinary guidelines for our failure to comply. Finally, Christian ethics establishes an eternal standard. The

---

37. H. Gardner, *Intelligence Reframed*, p. 57, Basic Books.

completeness of the lessons from the mountainside oratory of Jesus is astounding. Its simplicity is beautiful. Its lesson compelling. We are to be as gracious and merciful as our Lord. Forgive the transgressions against us, turn away from evil, and offer the other cheek. Holy in every thought and appearance is our aspiration.

Bart C. Craytor is an attorney with Dunbar, Craytor & Morgan in Texarkana, Texas. He holds BS and MAS from Southeastern Oklahoma State University, and the JD from Oklahoma City University School of Law.

11

Accounting, Finance, and Economics

"Know well the condition of your flock,
and pay attention to your herds."
—Prov. 27:23

"Serve wholeheartedly,
as if you were serving the Lord, not men."
—Eph. 6:7 NIV

"Use honest scales and honest weights,
an honest ephah and an honest hin.
I am the LORD your God, who brought you out of Egypt."
—Lev. 19:36 NIV

"We are never really happy
until we try to brighten the lives of others."
—Helen Keller

"Learn to say no; it will be of more use to you
than to be able to read Latin."
—Charles Spurgeon

"Though I am always in haste, I am never in a hurry because I never undertake more work than I can go through with calmness of spirit."
—John Wesley

"Alone we can do so little; together we can do so much."
—Helen Keller

A Biblical Basis for Accounting

Rodney Allen Oglesby

THE ACCOUNTING profession has experienced major challenges in the past few years: the demise of Arthur Andersen, the SEC promulgation of new rules and requirements, and the passage of the Sarbanes-Oxley Act. Each action indicates that the profession is under attack and the actions of both public and private accountants are being scrutinized more than ever before.

The demise of Arthur Andersen, World-Com, and the scandal at Tyco have posed a significant challenge to the stature of the accounting profession and raised questions about the ethical choices of both the auditor (public CPA) and/or the corporate accountant (corporate CPA or CMA). Many pundits have called the actions of the auditors or corporate accountants as "unethical," violating the ethical code of the American Institute of Certified Public Accountants (AICPA) or the Institute of Management Accountants (IMA). In 1998 Arthur Levitt, Chairman of the SEC, spoke on accounting issues at New York University's Center for Law and Business. Levitt expressed concern over corporate earnings management. Responding to corporate charges of misconduct Levitt promised that the SEC would "[R]oot out and aggressively act on abuses of the financial reporting process"[1] President George W. Bush, in a speech in Manhattan, stated ". . . America's greatest economic need is higher ethical standards." He went further to add that there was a need for a new ". . . era of integrity in corporate America." The *integrity* foundation of the accounting profession has been shaken.[2] Additionally there has been a developing position, when examining the applicability of accounting to religious thought, that financial ". . . accounting and accountability matters are seen as secular and secondary."[3] Further,

---

1. Remarks by Chairman Arthur Levitt, Securities and Exchange Commission—The Numbers Game," NYU Center for Law and Business, September 28, 1998; retrieved from http://www.sec.gov/news/speech/speecharchive/1998/spch220.txt on November 12, 2007.

2. Bush, G. W. "Transcript of President's Address Calling for New Era of Corporate Integrity. New York Times." (New York, New York, 2002), July 10, C-4.

3. Laughlin, R. "A Model of Financial Accountability and the Church of England."

Booth (1993) recorded that accounting is "... seen as ... [a] secular ... activity."[4] If accounting is secular, then where is the biblical basis for accounting? In actuality there is a plethora of references in the Bible to being accountable and providing accountability. There is significant importance attached to keeping accounts (tracking activities) and being accountable in the relationships among all of God's children.

The Law

The Pentateuch (Genesis through Deuteronomy) has a great deal of teaching and law related to conducting moral business practices. As an agricultural society, these laws and principles may seem to be unrelated to the challenges of the technologically advanced cultures of today. However, the teachings and principles of the Bible have a way of transcending time and environments.

The First Accountant?

Genesis provides our first exposure to a *bean counter*. When speaking of Joseph, scripture records "[I]t came to pass on a certain day, when he went into the house to do his business . . ." (Gen. 39:11 NIV). One translation of this passage indicates that the *business* to which Joseph was to attend was to examine the book of accounts. Later, Joseph was placed in charge of Egypt's food supply and through his skillful management, and examination of accounts, Egypt was to survive seven years of famine. Joseph was an excellent accountant!

The First Audit

Moses also desired "accurate records" reporting on activities of the construction of the Tabernacle, commanding that an accounting be made. "This is the sum of the tabernacle, even of the tabernacle of testimony, as it was counted, according to the commandment of Moses . . ." (Exod. 38:21–31 NIV) The Israelites had contributed significant funds (Exodus 38:21–31 indicates the form of money employed included talents and shekels) for the construction of the Tabernacle. In order to assure the Israelites that no stealing of resources or misappropriation had occurred, Moses commanded a full accounting of all contributions and expenditures. Note specifically that Moses may have served as the treasurer but

Financial Accounting and Management. Vol. 6 Num 2, 95–114.

    4. Booth, P. "Accounting in Churches: A Research Framework and Agenda." *Accounting, Auditing and Accountability Journal*, Vol. 6, No. 4, 37–67.

the accounting was made by Ithamar, and the first independent audit was conducted and reported to the public!

The Underlying Principles

The Ten Commandments provide the foundation of the auditing principles followed today. Do not lie. Do not deceive one another. Do not swear falsely. Do not defraud your neighbor. Judge your neighbor fairly. All of these support the objective that accountants and auditors present fairly the financial performance of a company. Using Moses as an example, we all should strive to be above suspicion, to be objective, to maintain independence in our financial reporting. Above all, the financial dealings should be communicated truthfully.

The concept of a fair presentation of financial performance is also supported in Leviticus: "Do not use dishonest standards when measuring length, weight or quantity. Use honest scales and honest weights" (Lev. 19:35 NIV). The process of accounting for a business must be performed following generally accepted accounting principles (honest standards) not the dishonest standards we've seen followed in several of the financial debacles of the last decade. Only through the use of honest measures can owners and investors make accurate assessments and informed choices.

We can extend the honest measure to the area of deceptive reporting of financial information. If accountants are not reporting the truth (massaging the financial statements to improve the corporation's financial performance), then they mislead investors and creditors and are guilty of being dishonest. Investors and creditors must be able to depend upon the financial statements in making investment/financial decisions.

Call for Accountability

Although, the Pentateuch provides a great deal of instruction on the practice of ethics in business and accounting, the New Testament also has lessons for us all. Luke 16:8–9 suggests that Christians should use and manage their resources wisely. Accounting is necessary to manage our resources and be accountable for that which God entrusts to us. In Matthew 25:14, the parable of the talents reinforces the responsibility we have to be accountable for that which our master places with us. The use of the word, *master* includes our employer as well as our Lord. Luke 16:2 further emphasizes that accounting is important. A rich man is told that his manager is wasting his possessions. The rich man asks the manager to give an account of his management. This illustrates that only by tracking the results of our actions can we provide a proper accounting of our actions.

Mercantile Transactions

From the early exchange of animal skins for grain to today's computerized transfers of electronic assets for electronic credits, accountants, and accounting procedures have been an integral link in the recording and reporting of business or exchange transactions. Accounting as an activity has been around as long as humans have exchanged goods and services. Whether it is to assist in tracking a medium of exchange (one shekel is equal to one ox), sales or inventory by recording marks on a clay tablet or through the tying of knots on a cord, accounting created a history (in financial or volume terms) of transactions for managers and owners. Accounting has evolved along with the changes in the speed and complexity of transactions developing an abstract semantic language to track transactions. Double entry accounting surfaced in the thirteenth century and still serves us well today.

Commitments for the Future

As we look to the Bible for guidance on accounting and consider how we must function to be in keeping with Scriptural views, it is clear that there is a strong basis in the Bible for the field of accounting provided we follow biblical principles including:

- Auditors should be completely independent outsiders and distance themselves from false matters,

- Accountants must hold to the highest ethical behavior,
  — Do not steal,
  — Do not deny falsely,
  — Do not lie to one another,
  — Do not swear falsely.

If the auditors and consultants from Arthur Andersen and the Enron accounting staff had performed their accounting services in accordance with the principles above, then the challenges the profession currently faces would not exist. What is needed in the profession is a stronger commitment to the biblical teaching regarding accounting and accountability.

Rodney Allen Oglesby is a Professor of Accounting at Drury University. He holds the BS from the University of Missouri-Columbia, an MBA from Southern Illinois and the PhD from the University of Missouri-Columbia. He holds certifications including the CPA, CMA, CFM, Certified Government Financial Manager and Certified Valuation Analyst.

Finance
Toward a Biblical Worldview

Tom D. Stevens

SHOULD A biblical worldview change the way we practice finance? A quick glance at the landscape of finance in practice today reveals preferences among financial managers to focus primarily on shareholder wealth at the detriment of stakeholder well-being and short-term profitability at the cost of long-term sustainability. For the Christian finance professional, these practices are called into question. Although we should not throw aside modern finance theory in order to fulfill our call to love our neighbor and to love God, we should seek to understand how a biblical worldview can shape our practice of finance. The following biblical perspectives are a starting point in this pursuit.

Perspective 1
Finance is Part of God's Natural Order.

First and foremost, it is vital that we recognize finance not as a secular invention created to advance the riches of the powerful and oppress the poor and enslaved. Instead, finance should be understood as part of the natural order that God created ex nihilo for the benefit of his creation and to His glory.[5] When used for the glory of God and the service of our neighbors, money helps to "bring resources together in the correct time and place and helps us to see the value of different resources as we make choices about which activities to conduct."[6] In fact, some would argue that money will continue to serve this function in the new heavens and new earth as we reign with Christ and interact with one another eternally. In that sense, finance plays a critical role in the Kingdom of God both

---

5. Fr. Robert Sirico, "The Entrepreneurial Vocation," in *Beyond Integrity*, eds. Scott B. Rae and Kenman L. Wong (Grand Rapids, MI: Zondervan, 1996), 214.

6. Todd P. Steen, Steve VanderVeen and Julie Voskuil, "Finance: On Earth as It is in Heaven?" *Managerial Finance 32,* no. 10 (2006), 807.

in the present and future realities.[7] However, finance often falls short of its created intent because our love for God and love for our neighbors is misdirected towards a self-centered love for money (1 Tim. 6:10). Many of the recent financial scandals highlighted in the press are the result of an improper understanding of the role of finance and a misdirected love for money. Recognizing that finance is a part of God's natural order may help us to practice finance in a way that glorifies its Maker.

Perspective 2
The Pursuit of Excellence in Finance

As we come to discover finance as a part of God's created order, we should also be encouraged towards the pursuit of excellence in the theory and practice of finance. The great philosopher Etienne Gilson conveyed this truth powerfully writing, "If one wants to practice science for God's sake, the first condition is to practice it for its own sake, or as if for its own sake, because that is the only way to learn it. . . . It is the same with an art: one must have it before one can put it to God's service. We are told that faith built the medieval cathedrals; no doubt, but faith would not have built anything had there been no architects and craftsmen. We . . . who acclaim the high worth of nature because it is God's work, should show our respect for it by taking as our first rule of action that piety is never a substitute for technique; for technique is that without which the most fervent piety is powerless to make use of nature for God's sake."[8]

In the formation of the early church, the apostles selected "seven men of good reputation, full of the Spirit and of wisdom," to put in charge of serving the tables, which was a reference to the banks where funds and supplies were administered for widows.[9] The finance role carried out by these men enabled the apostles to devote themselves to "prayer and the ministry of the word." The ultimate result of this division of labor was that, "the word of God kept on spreading; and the number of the disciples continued to increase greatly in Jerusalem" (Acts 6:3–7).

Pursuing excellence in finance, whether in the church or in a large corporation, enables the creation of value that can be used for the service

---

7. Ibid., 802.

8. Fr. Robert Sirico, "The Entrepreneurial Vocation," in Beyond Integrity, eds. Scott B. Rae and Kenman L. Wong (Grand Rapids, MI: Zondervan, 1996), 214.

9. Stanley D. Toussaint, "Acts," in *The Bible Knowledge Commentary*, New Testament ed., eds. John F. Walvoord and Roy B. Zuck (Colorado Springs, CO: Cook Communications Ministries, 2000), 367.

of others and the glory of God. Take for example the decision made by UPS to reduce the number of left turns made by its trucks during deliveries. Managers at UPS recognized that left turns require additional time and fuel as trucks wait for oncoming cars to pass. Thus, UPS invested in the development of route optimization software that has ultimately led to 54.4 million gallons of fuel saved per year and the reduction of some 85,000 trucks and cars out of the logistics systems for all users of the software. [10] The pursuit of excellence in finance can create value to be shared among both stakeholders and owners, and ultimately glorifies the Creator of all things good (James 1:17).

Perspective 3
Balancing Profit Maximization and Stakeholder Relationships

We now turn to the issue of value maximization for shareholders at the detriment of stakeholders. Perhaps one of the greatest challenges in finance is balancing the investment goals of the owners with the needs and concerns of various stakeholders, even in the case of a sole proprietorship where the owner and manager are one in the same. According to the efficient markets hypothesis, it is in the best interest of the managers to protect the well-being of all stakeholders because the stakeholders' well-being will be incorporated into the investors' valuation of the firm. Yet, what happens when the owners hold extremely short-sighted views which essentially ignore long-term impacts on stakeholders?

The prophet Amos spoke with passion against the economic injustice of merchants in the northern kingdom of Israel, proclaiming, "Hear this, you who trample the needy, to do away with the humble of the land, saying, 'When will the new moon be over, so that we may sell grain, and the Sabbath, that we may open the wheat market, to make the bushel smaller and the shekel bigger, and to cheat with dishonest scales, so as to buy the helpless for money and the needy for a pair of sandals, and that we may sell the refuse of the wheat?'" (Amos 8:4–7 NASB).

God's compassion for the oppressed and His hatred for the oppressor have not changed. In fact, in the New Testament, we read time and time again that Christ came for the oppressed. In Luke as Jesus brought to life the words of Isaiah, proclaiming, "The Spirit of the Lord is upon me, because He anointed me to preach the gospel to the poor. He has sent me

---

10. Sarah Murray, "The Green Way to Keep on Trucking," *The Financial Times* [online], March 13, 2007.

to proclaim release to the captives, and recovery of sight to the blind, to set free those who are oppressed, to proclaim the favorable year of the Lord" (Luke 4:18–19 NASB).

This is not to say that it is the sole role of business to make God's Kingdom a reality on earth. However, these verses do speak to the value the Christian financial manager should attribute to various stakeholders, including customers, employees, and local communities. Although one should not abandon a value maximization strategy, it is important to include a proper view of stakeholders into value maximization models. In addition to profits, one should consider the "externalities imposed by profit maximizing choices on other stakeholders: on the welfare of management and workers who have invested their human capital as well as off-work related capital (housing, spouse employment, schools, social relationships, etc.) in the employment relationship; on suppliers and customers who also have sunk investments in the relationship and foregone alternative opportunities; on communities who suffer from the closure of a plant; and so forth."[11]

The God of the Bible is a relational God, and He views His world through a relational lens. Although finance is a science which defines reality according to what can be measured quantitatively, this should not allow the financial manager to ignore the relational components of his actions. While the livelihoods of families and communities may not always appear as *real* in financial models, behind the numbers are real people and real communities who deserve to be viewed as God views them, with love.

Recognizing the relational responsibility of the financial decision-maker does not dismiss him from his contractual obligation and responsibility to the owners and their shared set of values and expected goals. Rather, the relational consequences of the financial decision-maker's actions demand that he works harder to find a profit-maximizing solution which also values the concerns of the stakeholders. The fact that it is not easy is one of many reasons God instructs us to call upon Him often for wisdom and discernment (James 1:5).

Perspective 4
Finance is a Means of Stewardship

King David wrote in Psalm 24, "The earth is the Lord's and all it contains, the world, and those who dwell in it. For He has founded it upon the seas and established it upon the rivers" (Ps 24:1–2 NASB). Jesus built upon

---

11. Jean Tirole, "Corporate Governance," *Econometrica*, vol. 69, no. 1 (2001), 23.

this truth, teaching, "Therefore if you have not been faithful in the use of unrighteous wealth, who will entrust the true riches to you? And if you have not been faithful in the use of that which is another's who will give you that which is your own?" (Luke 16:11–12 NASB).

As Christians we are called to be good stewards of the earth and all that it contains. At least in part, finance fulfills this function in that it provides an efficient means of resource allocation. Allowing capital to flow to its most profitable use enables us to make resource allocation choices which would otherwise be nearly impossible. In fact, the woes of many developing economies are directly related to a lack of capital budgeting. The following excerpt from an article published in *The International Research Journal of Finance and Economics* speaks loudly to this issue: "Even in the midst of vast economic and resources [with] endowment, African countries are not only technologically backward but wallow in neck-deep poverty and indebtedness. . . In Nigeria, a preponderant majority of about over (sic) 100 million is in a situation of misrule, instability, poverty, hopelessness, corruption, moral decay, violence and general macro economic uncertainty. . . The solution to all these problems lies in the fact that firms are to embark on projects that would give rise to company's value which will by extension enhance the desired economic development for the country."[12] In the same way that finance serves to support economic development at the national level, finance also serves to provide development at the regional and local levels. Carrying out wise and biblical financing practices is part of fulfilling our role as stewards of God's earth and all that it contains.

Perspective 5: Stewardship Requires a Long-Term Perspective. A key principle in finance is the time value of money. In valuing an investment, cash flows received sooner are valued higher than cash flows received later due to the ability to reinvest cash and earn additional returns. Combine this basic principle with the fact that securities markets follow quarterly results and executives' compensation schemes reward short-term profits, and we should not be surprised that financial managers often have very short-sighted understandings of value. How does this short-sightedness relate to our call to be stewards of the earth?

In April of 2007, a group of executives from leading oil and manufacturing companies met in a high-rise building overlooking a surprisingly smog-free Hong Kong to discuss the role of business in addressing global

12. D. O. Elumilade, T. O. Asaolu and A. O. Ologunde, "Capital Budgeting and Economic Development in the Third World: The Case of Nigeria," *International Research Journal of Finance and Economics*, Issue 2 (2006), 136.

environmental threats. The round-table discussion was part of BBC's series on *The Business of Climate Control*. At the heart of the discussion was the concern that the pursuit of short-term financial goals by heavy carbon dioxide emitting companies could lead to long-term environmentally devastating consequences. In defense of their financial and strategic decisions, executives argued they were simply acting as agents on behalf of their shareholders. The mediator of the discussion called into question the scope of responsibility held by financial decision-makers, indicating that executives' responsibility extends to the long-term sustainability of the business and its environment.

A short review of the covenants of the Old Testament reveals the God of the Bible who establishes everlasting covenants with His people. In Genesis, chapter nine, God established a covenant with Noah which extended even to future generations of all the animals of earth. To Abraham God declared, "I will establish My covenant between Me and you and your descendants after you throughout their generations for an everlasting covenant, to be God to you and to your descendants after you" (Gen. 17:7 NASB). Thus, in seeking a biblical worldview for understanding the role of time in financial decision making, the Christian would be served well to consider the significant value God places not only on the present generation but future generations as well.

The Jewish Talmud provides a beautiful illustration of this concept in the following parable, "One day [a man] was journeying on the road and he saw [another] man planting a carob tree; he asked him, How long does it take [for this tree] to bear fruit? The man replied: Seventy years. He then further asked him: Are you certain that you will live another seventy years? The man replied: I found [ready grown] carob trees in the world; as my forefathers planted these for me so I too plant these for my children" (Soncino Talmud, Ta'anith 23a).[13]

Perspective 6
Finance is Not an End in Itself

In the pursuit of excellence in finance, it is important to remember that finance is not an end in itself. The parable of the rich man taught by Jesus in Luke 12 sets forth a strong reminder of this reality. Jesus began the parable saying, "The land of a rich man was very productive. And he began reason-

---

13. John Ray Initiative, "Environmental Christianity: Insights from our Jewish Heritage," *The JRI Briefing Papers*, No. 13, available from http://www.jri.org.uk/brief/Jewish_Insights.htm.

ing to himself, saying, 'What shall I do, since I have no place to store my crops?' Then he said, 'This is what I will do: I will tear down my barns and build larger ones, and there I will store all my grain and my goods. And I will say to my soul, "Soul, you have many goods laid up for many years to come: take your ease, eat, drink and be merry."' But God said to him, 'You fool! This very night your soul is required of you; and now who will own what you have prepared?' So is the man who stores up treasure for himself, and is not rich toward God" (Luke 12:16–21 NASB). Without question, the finance professional can serve God magnificently through the science of finance. Yet, the financial manager who pursues excellence in finance and reaps great profits for both stakeholders and shareholders but neglects to manage his own relationship with the almighty Creator with the same diligence will have failed most miserably.

Conclusion

Holding to a biblical worldview should shape the way we practice finance. While a biblical perspective does not preclude the pursuit of profit, even large profits, adhering to a biblical worldview does change the basic values used in decision making by financial managers. The biblical perspectives explored in this essay lead to both a greater sense of purpose in finance as well as a greater sense of responsibility in financial decision making. In light of the ever-present challenges facing the Christian finance professional, Fr. Robert Sirico provided the following encouragement, "In the pursuit of your vocation you will be tempted in many ways. You may be tempted to give up and think that the sometimes mundane world of finances, business and materialism has no spiritual dimension or meaning. Or perhaps you will be tempted in the opposite direction: to think that all that matters is the bottom line, and that no other values can have any bearing. In those moments, this priest prays that you will remember the Incarnation, and the cost that was paid by the Son of God in that freely chosen action to enter the material world and to sanctify it."[14] Indeed, finance practiced according to biblical principles can serve as one of many tools God has given His creation to take part in the sanctification of the material world.

Tom D. Stevens is an Instructor of Economics at Southwest Baptist University. He holds a BS from Southwest Baptist University, a MTS from Dallas Theological Seminary, and an MBA from Southern Methodist University.

14. Fr. Robert Sirico, "The Entrepreneurial Vocation," in *Beyond Integrity*, eds. Scott B. Rae and Kenman L. Wong (Grand Rapids, MI: Zondervan, 1996), 214–215.

Judeo-Christian Influences on Socio-economics

Marshal H. Wright and James R. Russell

The Heritage Foundation's *2002 Index of Economic Freedom* (Index) proposes that the degree of economic freedom present within any given country's socio-economic policies and activities will directly affect the standard and quality of living of that country's citizens.[15] The assertion is made that "most of the world's economically free countries are those with a rule of law and system of economic liberty inherited or adopted from the Anglo-Saxon capitalist model."[16] Recent trends support this assertion: "North America and Europe remain the world's most economically free [region], containing six of the top ten freest countries . . . .On net, the region shows a gain in economic freedom by four."[17] However, we propose that a more accurate assertion would be that the foundations of economic freedom can be better explained as a product of "a rule of law and system of economic liberty inherited or adopted from the . . . " Judeo-Christian socioeconomic model.

The *2002 Index of Economic Freedom* primarily focuses on the level of "government interference in the economy" that "influence[s] the institutional setting of economic growth" as a product of ten critical foundational criteria that, when viewed comprehensively, provide "an empirical photograph of a country's economic freedom"[18] leading to better living standards for its citizens. The ten critical criteria upon which the Index bases its ratings are: "Trade Policy, Fiscal Burden of Government, Government

---

15. *2002 Index of Economic Freedom.* Edited by G. P. O'Driscoll, Jr., K. R. Holmes, & M. A. O'Grady. New York, NY: The Heritage Foundation and Dow Jones & Company, Inc.

16. Feulner, Edwin, "Preface" *2002 Index of Economic Freedom.* Edited by G. P. O'Driscoll Jr., K. R. Holmes, & M. A. O'Grady. New York, NY: The Heritage Foundation and Dow Jones & Company, Inc., (2002) xiii–xiv.

17. "Executive Summary," *2002 Index of Economic Freedom.* Edited by G. P. O'Driscoll, Jr., K. R. Holmes, & M. A. O'Grady. New York, NY: The Heritage Foundation and Dow Jones & Company, Inc., (2002), 3.

18. Ibid., 1.

Intervention in the Economy, Monetary Policy, Capital Flows and Foreign Investment, Banking and Finance, Wages and Prices, Property Rights, Regulation, and Black Market."[19] In the 2002 Index, it has been proffered by Hoskins and Eiras that "Property rights" (understood from a broad socio-economic policy perspective) is the central element, or criterion, around which all of the other criteria revolve. They conclude that:

> The extent to which governments carry out their responsibility to respect and protect property rights does much to determine the extent to which economic growth is possible and individuals can use freely what is theirs and enjoy the things that science, technology, and innovation can deliver to improve their lives.[20]

All of the other criteria are focused on regulations and activities (both governmental and individual) that revolve around and affect the ability of individuals to "make the most efficient use of what they own, which in turn promotes economic growth and prosperity for all."[21] Therefore, it can be concluded that the other nine criteria, in summary, affect the individual use, transferability, and enjoyment of property resources, which is the primary measurement of socio-economic freedom as a predictor of economic growth and an improved socio-economic condition.

The *free* and *mostly free* designations of the *2002 Index of Economic Freedom* rest heavily upon a socio-economic philosophy that emphasizes the role of the individual operating in a free-market competitive environment. The Heritage Foundation Index rankings are solidly based upon the foundational philosophical emphases on governmental restraint, individual self-interest, and free market competitive individualism.

In contrast, the *mostly unfree* and *repressed* designations of the *2002 Index of Economic Freedom* rest heavily upon a philosophy that emphasizes significant imposition of governmental socio-economic intervention and restraint of the role of the individual and free-market competition. This socio-economic philosophy is explained well by Hayek's commentary on *socialist collectivism*. Hayek identifies socialist collectivism in action as "the abolition of private enterprise, of private ownership of the means of production, and the creation of a system of 'planned economy' in which the

19. "Executive Summary," *2002 Index of Economic Freedom*. Edited by G. P. O'Driscoll, Jr., K. R. Holmes, & M. A. O'Grady. New York, NY: The Heritage Foundation and Dow Jones & Company, Inc. (2002), p. 1.

20. Ibid., 37.

21. Hoskins, Lee & Eiras, Ana. "Property Rights: The Key to Economic Growth." *2002 Index of Economic Freedom*. Edited by G. P. O'Driscoll, Jr., K. R. Holmes, & M. A. O'Grady, (2002), 37.

entrepreneur working for profit is replaced by a central planning body."[22] According to this view, the actions of unrestrained and uncoordinated individuals are insufficient to create, maintain, and grow an efficient and effective socio-economic system. The Heritage Foundation Index rankings of *mostly unfree* and *repressed* are grounded upon the foundational philosophical emphases expressed in the restraint of individual socio-economic competitive action through the primary imposition of governmental interventions and central planning and control.

As stated previously, Lee Hoskins and Ana Eiras proffer that property rights (understood from a broad socio-economic policy perspective) is the central element, or criterion, around which all of the other criteria revolve in the *2002 Index of Economic Freedom*; and furthermore, all of the other criteria in the *Index* are focused on regulations and activities (both governmental interventions and individual responses) that revolve around and affect the ability of individuals to "make the most efficient use of what they own, which in turn promotes economic growth and prosperity for all."[23] According to this view, the functional role that private property/capital plays in any given interactive socio-economic system is a key variable that determines economic freedom and an improved socio-economic condition. This assertion is consistent with Judeo-Christian teachings of ownership of property and socio-economic activity.

Scripture provides support for a Judeo-Christian worldview approach to business and economics that emphasizes the ownership of private property and an intentional individual restraining of self-interest with the specific aim of working toward the common good. "Let him labor, working with his hands what is good, that he may have something to give him who has need" (Eph. 4:28 NKJV). In Acts we read, "I have shown you in every way, by laboring like this, that you must support the weak. And remember the words of the Lord Jesus, that He said, 'It is more blessed to give than to receive'" (Acts 20:35 NKJV). Luke adds, "'And even now the axe is laid to the root of the trees. Therefore, every tree which does not bear good fruit is cut down and thrown into the fire.' So the people asked him, saying, 'What shall we do then?' He answered and said to them, 'He who has two tunics, let him give to him who has none; and he who has food, let him do likewise'" (Luke 3:9–11 NKJV).

22. Hayek, Friedrich. *The Road to Serfdom*. Chicago, IL: The University of Chicago Press, (1994), 37.

23. Hoskins, Lee & Eiras, Ana, "Property Rights: The Key to Economic Growth," *2002 Index of Economic Freedom*. Edited by G. P. O'Driscoll Jr., K. R. Holmes, & M. A. O'Grady, (2002), 37.

The framework for the application of socio-economic activity practiced for the common good is provided by biblical Judeo-Christian teachings that espouse the Ten Commandments as the informational centerpiece of political-legal, socio-economic activity. The Ten Commandments (Exod. 20:1–17) present a governing framework guiding individual activity that has a three-fold focus: a) the relationship of individuals to God (verses 1–11), b) the relationship of individuals to each other (verses 12–14, 16–17), and c) the relationship of individuals to property—private property is sanctioned by God (verses 15, 17).

In Exodus 20:1–11, humankind is commanded to interact with, and acknowledge the existence of, the one and only transcendent and objective God who is a deliverer, is supreme, the Creator of all, who acts out of mercy toward those that conduct their affairs out of love and in accordance with His standards that are observable and which may be complied with. Verses 12–14, and 16–17 provide that individuals are expected to act with an appreciation for and sensitivity toward others (to be "other oriented") as a result of a basic understanding of God-created human dignity. This concept of being "other oriented" is applied not only to individuals personally, but it is also extended within the framework of private property. Verses 15 and 17 specifically admonish that individuals are not to covet or steal. This admonishment implicitly recognizes private ownership of property that carries with it rights and responsibilities in a human interactive context. Exodus 22:1–15 further expounds upon these fundamental principles of human interaction relative to private property and provides a platform (within a Judeo-Christian framework) for a political-legal, socio-economic system that, respects and protects property rights, and in turn, "does much to determine the extent to which economic growth is possible and individuals can use freely what is theirs and enjoy the things that science, technology, and innovation can deliver to improve their lives."[24]

As is evident, socio-economics viewed from the Judeo-Christian model perspective is practiced with an attitude of acknowledgement that God is, that He has placed into effect observable standards/principles of socio-economic human interaction that emphasize ownership, enjoyment, and use of private property in ways that are designed to encourage activity toward the common good, and that individual's interactive endeavors in the socio-economic realm should reflect His presence by practicing and applying these standards and principles.

24. Hoskins, Lee & Eiras, Ana, "Property Rights: The Key to Economic Growth," *2002 Index of Economic Freedom*. Edited by G. P. O'Driscoll, Jr., K. R. Holmes, & M. A. O'Grady, (2002), 37.

Part II: A Matter of Worldview

"Human beings were made in the image of God, to reflect His character; therefore, we are called to reflect His creative activity through our own creativity—by cultivating the world, drawing out its potential, and giving it shape and form. All work has dignity as an expression of the divine image."[25] This concept provides that economics should be practiced with a view toward the stewardship of property responsibilities that humankind has to God and in turn to fellow humankind that encourage economic growth and an improved socio-economic condition through an absolute truth morality-based philosophy of socio-economic activity.

In summary, the criteria items contained in the Heritage Foundation's *2002 Index of Economic Freedom* rankings, for the most part, are produced out of a Judeo-Christian model philosophy that encourages a Lockean approach to government restraint and protection of individuals' inherent rights and freedoms, including those related to the use, possession and enjoyment by individuals of private property.[26] The fundamental premise is that control of socio-economic activity is better done at the individual level when the mind and heart are controlled (or at least influenced) by God's interaction and intervention in individuals' lives (rather than by government intervention).

Using the CIA's fact book (Central Intelligence Agency), a study was conducted by Wright and Russell in which economic, demographic, and religious data were collected for each of the 156 countries included in the Heritage Foundation's Index of Economic Freedom (The Heritage Foundation). Specific data included predominant religion, gross domestic product per capita, and life expectancy. The data were then included with the Index of Economic Freedom to perform a cluster analysis. Examination of cluster centroids indicated that countries whose primary religions are Protestant, Catholic, Jewish and Indigenous enjoyed more economic freedom (index of economic freedom of 2.726 versus 3.359), have a higher standard of living (gross domestic product per capita of $10,723 versus $4,897), and a longer life expectancy (66.5 years versus 64.9 years).[27]

Among the conclusions drawn from the analysis is that the Judeo/Christian tradition was shown to be associated with greater economic free-

---

25. Colson, Charles & Pearcey, Nancy, *How Now Shall We Live?* Wheaton, Illinois: Tyndale House Publishers, Inc. (1999), 384.

26. Hoskins, Lee & Eiras, Ana, "Property Rights: The Key to Economic Growth," *2002 Index of Economic Freedom*. Edited by G. P. O'Driscoll, Jr., K. R. Holmes, & M. A. O'Grady, (2002), 37.

27. Wright and Russell, *A Global Analysis of the Economic Benefits of the Judeo-Christian Socio-Economic Model*, pending publication (2007).

dom, higher per capita GDP, and longer life expectancy. Results classify 100 % of the countries whose predominant religion is Protestant, Catholic or Jewish, into the cluster associated with greater economic freedom, higher per capita GDP, and a higher life expectancy are unlikely to be a statistical abnormality. A similar conclusion can be drawn from the classification of 100 % of the countries whose predominant religion is Muslim, Hindu and Non-religious into the cluster associated with less economic freedom, lower per capita GDP, and a shorter life expectancy.

However, the analysis also raises many unanswered questions. For example, is the fact that two clusters ended up being the optimal number of clusters significant or is it a statistical abnormality? Why are one hundred percent of the countries whose predominant religion is indigenous and 30 % of the Buddhist countries grouped in Cluster 1 associated with more economic freedom, a higher standard of living, and a higher life expectancy? Could Hong Kong, whose predominant religion is indigenous, which has the most economic freedom, and which has one of the highest per capita GDP's, be skewing the results? Could countries, whose predominant religion is Buddhist but still have a significant number of Christians, be biasing the results? Why are one hundred percent of the countries, whose predominant religion is Christian Orthodox, grouped in Cluster 2 associated with less economic freedom, a lower per capita GDP, and a lower life expectancy? Is the reason statistical, historical, political, or theological? The answers to these and many more questions must be left for further analysis.

As stated previously, the criteria items contained in the Heritage Foundation's *2002 Index of Economic Freedom* rankings, for the most part, are produced out of a Judeo-Christian model philosophy that encourages a Lockean approach to government restraint and protection of individuals' inherent rights and freedoms, including those related to the use, possession and enjoyment by individuals of private property.[28] The fundamental premise is that control of socio-economic activity is better done on the individual level when the mind and heart are controlled (or at least influenced) by God's intervention in individuals' lives (rather than by government intervention).

We would propose that in countries where there has been an historical development of socio-economic structures grounded in a model of Judeo-Christian influence, the result has been greater levels of applied morality and God ordained and empowered individual self-restraint that

---

28. Hoskins, Lee & Eiras, Ana, "Property Rights: The Key to Economic Growth," *2002 Index of Economic Freedom.* Edited by G. P. O'Driscoll, Jr., K. R. Holmes, & M. A. O'Grady, (2002), 37.

results in less need for government intervention and an attending increase in socio-economic freedom, growth and an improved socio-economic condition. This is a socio-economic approach that is truly consistent with the economic philosophies contained within the Index's model.

In that regard it is also proposed that, as other countries around the world (that do not come out of the Judeo-Christian socio-economic tradition) adopt this socio-economic model, the result will be greater and greater socio-economic freedom, growth, and an improved socio-economic condition as indicated by the recent global trend toward economic freedom documented in The Heritage Foundation's *2002 Index of Economic Freedom*. If this is true, a reasonable alternative query would be: If freedom and an improved socio-economic condition are associated with structures that have been historically built upon the Judeo-Christian model, will those countries that leave those foundations (Europe and the United States?) start to decline in their freedom and socio-economic positioning? In this regard, it should be anecdotally noted that many would argue that the recent history of the United States is one that is becoming more and more secular and/or anti Judeo-Christian. The linkage between our own nation's Judeo-Christian heritage and greater socio-economic freedom, growth and improved conditions is worthy of consideration and further research.

Marshal H. Wright is a Professor of Business at Oral Roberts University. He has a BS and MBA from Oral Roberts University and the JD and PhD from Regent University.

James R. Russell is Chair of Undergraduate Business Studies and Professor of Business at Oral Roberts University. He holds his BS and Masters from Oklahoma State University and a PhD from Virginia Tech University.

Economics: A Biblical Perspectives

Shawn Ritenour

MANY CHRISTIANS are surprised when they discover how relevant God's Word is for economics. God created a material world over which we are to have dominion, and He gave us minds to discover principles to guide us in doing so. There are way too many economic principles implied by Scripture to be adequately covered in one essay. In this essay, we will have to be content elaborating only a few of the most important.

Genesis is rightly called the book of beginnings. Not only does the word *Genesis* itself mean beginning, but the foundation of knowledge concerning so many issues of our life is found there as well. This foundation includes the basis for all scientific inquiry, including economics. From the very first chapter, we find that we are in a teleological universe. God made all things for a purpose and gave man the first commandment to have dominion over the earth. We are called to do this, however, in our present, fallen, and finite world with a scarcity of means. Since our banishment from the Garden of Eden, man has faced a central cultural dilemma: how do we fulfill God's creation mandate in a world of aggravated scarcity without either starving to death or killing one another.

This is not at all a moot point. Whether they know it or not, different societies seek to answer this question with every change of economic institutions and policies. History is full of stark examples revealing that different attempts to solve our dilemma have resulted in widely different consequences. Economic theory rooted in an understanding of man as a rational actor created in God's image teaches that to materially fulfill God's cultural mandate, we must take advantage of the division of labor, capital accumulation, and entrepreneurship. These three pillars of economic development require societal maintenance of the biblical ethic of private property.

The Cultural Mandate

Even before sin and the fall of man, God told our first parents to be fruitful and multiply, replenish the earth, subdue it, and have dominion over every living thing that moves upon the earth. In the second chapter of Genesis we find our first father being called to work and keep the Garden. The cultural mandate, then, requires filling, working, keeping, and ruling creation.[29] It requires filling the earth with people, making real concrete changes in nature, exercising dominion over all creation, but also doing so in a way that will not destroy and waste, but protect and replenish. Fulfilling God's dominion mandate, therefore, requires wise balance. It is possible that we rashly try to draw too much from creation too quickly, make changes too abruptly, or do so without replenishing the earth. We can, however, err on the other extreme and act as if nature is a museum and we are its curator.

In light of the cultural mandate and the nature of the cursed ground, two questions come to the forefront. How do we develop God's creation wisely? How do we fill the earth with people without our starving to death or killing one another in a barbaric struggle for survival? It should be apparent that multiplying the population and subduing and exercising dominion over the earth requires economic progress. Fulfilling the cultural mandate obviously requires survival. It further necessitates each person developing his or her potential and the development of the potential of the natural order.

The Created Order, the Nature of Man, and Economics

In order for economics to help us identify how we can wisely exercise dominion in supporting a growing population, we must look to an economics that is a sound reflection of reality. That is to say that we must root our economic investigations in a biblical understanding of the created order and the nature of man. Christian doctrine derived from the biblical record reveals that economics as a social science is something that can be pursued with confidence. If we are intellectually careful and if we begin with the right biblical presuppositions, we can discover certain absolute truths about how humans interact with each other via voluntary exchange.

Economics is a social science. If we are to discover economic truth, consequently, we must first be able to undertake science in general and must second be able to discover universal truths regarding social interac-

---

29. On the nature of the cultural mandate see Hegeman, David Bruce, *Plowing in Hope: Toward a Biblical Theology of Culture*, (Moscow, Idaho: Canon Press, 1999), 41–47 and Gordon, T. David and Jeffrey M. Herbener, "The Entrepreneurial Vocation." Unpublished Manuscript, (2004).

tion. Thankfully, the universe that God created allows us to do both. The biblical view of science recognizes that God is the maker of heaven and earth and of all things visible and invisible. All existence and all knowledge, consequently, have their source in God. When we say "all knowledge," this includes all facts, creature characteristics, and scientific laws. We know that we can undertake science for two reasons: God has created and continues to sustain a universe with certain regularities that can be discovered. God has made our mind so that we have the ability to discover such regularities.

In the very opening chapter of Genesis, we are told that God created the universe with purpose and order. We are told that God created and actively sustains the universe (Gen. 1:1; Col. 1:16–17; Heb. 1:3). The universe God created is one of purpose and order.[30] God made the sun, moon, and stars to exist for a purpose (Gen. 1:14–17). God made every animal to produce after its kind (Gen. 1:20–25). The order is so recognizable that God uses the regular recurrences of the seasons and of night and day and the endurance and stability of creation as evidence that we can rely on Him to keep His covenant (Jer. 33:20–21, Ps. 119:89–90; 72:5–7, 17; 89:34–37).[31] Because God created a universe with order and purpose, we can undertake science. There are cause and effect regularities in the created order to be discovered by man.

The Christian view of man begins with the fact that man is created by God in His image (Gen. 1:27). Part of the image of God is cognitive faculties. God thinks (Isa. 55:8–9; Jer. 29:11). God is rational. "Come now, let us reason together, says the Lord" (Isa. 1:18). God is also omniscient (Ps. 139:1–6). As a being created in God's image, man possesses mental faculties he can use to know things. God made us with minds that reflect His image. With our minds we are able to perceive reality because the same Creator who made our minds made the world in a way that harmonizes with our mental categories. God has made us with the ability to know and discover truth. It is true that we are finite, so we cannot know exhaustive knowledge. We can, however, know some truth with certainty (John 5:13). Part of truth that we can know with certainty is the regularities in the created order. Such cause and effect regularities are called scientific laws.

Economics is a social science in that it studies how humans interact through voluntary exchange. As such, the object of our study in economics

30. North, Gary. *The Dominion Covenant*. Tyler, Texas: The Institute for Christian Economics, (1987), 12–26.

31. Jaki, Stanley L., *The Savior of Science*, (Washington, D.C.: Regnery Gateway, (1998), 56–66.

is man. A sound economics, then, must build upon a sound understanding of man. The Christian doctrine of the nature of man also has much to tell us about economics. We have already noted that man is created in God's image. We understand more about the nature of man, then, as we understand more about the image of God. Christians understand the *image of God* to mean God's likeness. We can learn something about the nature of man, therefore, by examining the attributes of God. For the purposes of the subject of economics, it is sufficient to stress only a few characteristics of God as revealed in the Bible. As noted earlier, God thinks and He also plans (Eph. 1:4, 5). Not only does God think, but He acts as well. Within only the first four verses of Genesis, we learn that God created, spoke, and divided. All of these are actions. Moreover, God specifically acts with a purpose. God created the sun, moon, and stars in order to serve as signs, seasons, days, and years, and to give light to the earth (Gen. 1:14–17).

Because God thinks and acts with purpose and because man is made in the image of God, it is reasonable to conclude that man is able to think and act with purpose. It can be inferred, then, that a very important part of the image of God is reason: the ability to think rationally, in terms of cause and effect. Additionally, the Bible explicitly reveals man to be a creature who also thinks and acts with a purpose. In the Bible we find God the Father and Christ the Son dealing with man in a rational manner (Isa. 1:18; Matt. 8:5–8). Scripture also indicates that in acting, people routinely apply means to satisfy their ends. The Apostle Paul explicitly recognizes that things in this world are used by people as means to achieve ends (1 Cor. 7:31). When the Bible records King Solomon's importation of goods from various foreign countries, the original Hebrew explicitly refers to the silver coins used to buy the merchandise as the "open hand" an idiom meaning the power by which one can achieve something. For Solomon, money was the *means* by which he obtained the linen, chariot, and horses he wanted (1 Kings 10:28–29; 2 Chron. 1:16–17).[32]

The Christian doctrine of man instructs us that man was created in God's image and, as such, he is a being who engages in purposeful behavior. Humans engage in action. We are not inanimate objects merely responding to outside stimuli and we are not mere biological organisms driven by instincts and primeval urges. We are beings equipped for dominion by being given a mind and will with which we can think and act. Any sound biblical economics must take full account of the fact that a defining

---

32. Strong, James, *Hebrew and Chaldee Dictionary Accompanying the Exhaustive Concordance* in *Strong's Exhaustive Concordance*, (Gordonsville, Tennessee: Dugan Publishers, Incorporated), 47.

feature of man is that he engages in action. Sound economics begins with the truth that man acts, and, because this is a feature of our bearing God's image, it is a universal trait amongst human beings. Consequently, if we begin with the axiom that humans act, we can use the laws of logic to deduce true economic laws.[33] As long as we do not make any mistakes in our logic, our conclusions must be true because our beginning premise is rooted in the authority of Scripture, which we know to be true. Therefore, the biblical view of the created order and the nature of man allows us to undertake economic inquiry with the confidence that the economic laws we discover will be universally true for all people for all time.

Human Action and the Foundations of Economics

Action is applying means according to ideas to achieve an end. An end is the goal or motive for acting.[34] From the biblical view of man as a purposeful actor, we can deduce the concepts of value, cost, profit, and loss. An existential fact of life is that people have more ends than they have means to achieve those ends. Our means, therefore, are scarce. Even in the Garden of Eden, Adam and Eve presumably could not be at the same place at the same time and they could not do two things at once. Adam could not at the same time be planting soybeans in one corner of the Garden and naming vertebrate animals in another. The curse of the Fall did not create scarcity, but aggravated it a great deal. No longer would the earth naturally bring forth bountiful fruit. It would bring forth thorns and thistles. Man has to work harder cultivating the ground, clearing weeds and husbanding flowers and plants. We now eat bread, as Genesis reminds us, by the sweat of our brow.

Because means are scarce, we cannot achieve all of our possible ends. Therefore, we must choose to achieve some ends and leave others unfulfilled. Ranking ends necessitates preference, so we must conclude that action implies valuation. When acting we demonstrate that we prefer satisfying some ends more than others. Having to act to satisfy some ends

---

33. The method of deducing economic laws from human action is called praxeological. For more on Praxeology as the method of economics see Rothbard, Murray, "The Mantle of Science" in *The Logic of Action One: Money, Method, and the Austrian School*, by Edward Elgar, (1997), 3–23 and Mises, Ludwig von, *The Ultimate Foundation of Econmic Science*, (Kansas City, Missouri: Sheed Andrews and McMeel, Inc. 1962).

34. On the first principles of human action see Rothbard, Murray, *Man, Economy, and State with Power and Market* (Auburn, Alabama: The Ludwig von Mises Institute, 2005), p. 1–77, and Mises, Ludwig von, *Human Action*, Scholars Edition, (Auburn, Alabama: The Ludwig von Mises Institute, 1998), 1–143.

and leave others unfulfilled implies the concepts of benefit and cost and also profit and loss. The benefit of any action is the satisfaction one attains as a result of doing the action. The cost of any action is the value of the alternative that was not chosen. Choosing to act based on one's preferences implies the concepts of benefit and cost and also profit and loss.

Early in human history man, using the mind that God had given him, recognized the socially beneficial nature of exchange. People could increase their satisfaction and further their efforts in exercising dominion by trading with each other. All parties in exchange demonstrate that they value what they receive in an exchange more highly than what they give away, so that trade is mutually beneficial. We will find that exchange is also very beneficial to all of society, because it opens the door to the division of labor.

Economic Development

Fulfilling the cultural mandate requires sustaining a growing population that requires economic development. Economic theory identifies three sources necessary for economic progress: the division of labor, capital accumulation, and entrepreneurship. The division of labor opens the door to increased productivity by allowing people to specialize at lines of production where they are most efficient.[35] This increased productivity results in higher real incomes and increased societal wealth. However, people can only benefit from the division of labor if they are free to exchange the goods that they produce.

The use of capital goods contributes to economic progress by increasing the productivity of the user.[36] However, before capital goods can be used, they must be produced. In order to accumulate capital, people must be willing to put off present consumption so that they will have resources available to invest in production of capital goods. The higher people's time preferences are, the more present-oriented they are. They are less likely to save and invest, so they produce fewer capital goods, yielding less pro-

---

35. On the importance of the division of labor for economic and social development see Mises, *Human Action*, p. 624–682, Rothbard, "Freedom, Inequality, Primitivism, and the Division of Labor," in *The Logic of Action Two: Applications and Criticism from the Austrian School*, (Cheltenham, UK: Edward Elgar, 1997), 3–35.

36. On capital formation and its contribution to increased productivity and economic prosperity, see Rothbard, *Man, Economy and State with Power and Market*, 47–70, 517–27; Mises, "Capital and American Prosperity," in *Planning for Freedom and Sixteen Other Essays and Addresses* (South Holland, Illinois: Libertarian Press, 1980), 195–214; and Heurta de Soto, Jesus, *Money, Bank Credit, and Economic Cycles*, (Auburn, Alabama: The Ludwig von Mises Institute, 2006), 265–41.

ductive labor. The lower people's time preferences are, the more they will save and invest, accumulating more capital goods, resulting in increased productivity, incomes, and wealth. Likewise, with more capital investment comes better technology that will further increase productivity.

In order for economic progress to continue over time, however, it is important not to waste capital that has already been accumulated, which is why entrepreneurship is the third major contributor to economic development. Waste is possible, because production decisions in the present are based on a forecast of uncertain future market conditions. If the producer forecasts incorrectly, he will use his capital making something people do not want and will not be able to sell his output at the price needed to cover his costs.[37]

Entrepreneurs need to use economic calculation if they are to direct factors of production toward their most valued uses.[38] Market prices allow entrepreneurs to make meaningful comparisons of social value between different consumers' and producers' goods because money and price are all expressed in terms of the same good. These same objective prices are determined by the subjective preferences of buyers and sellers. If the expected price of a final product is greater than the sum of the prices of the factors of production, the entrepreneur will produce that good. When entrepreneurs reap a profit, they do it precisely by providing those goods that people value the most in the least costly manner.

One cannot neatly sever the components responsible for economic expansion from one another and find a single key that explains economic progress. A highly developed division of labor would be impossible without the accumulation and use of capital goods. Likewise, the entrepreneur must invest real capital in the production process and if he errs in his market forecast, he can indeed reap large losses. At the same time, capital *per se* never guarantees economic progress either, because it must be wisely utilized. Economic progress is the happy consequence of a highly developed division of labor, taking advantage of an increasing capital stock wisely invested by entrepreneurs. Consequently, if we want society to benefit from economic expansion, we need social institutions that foster the

---

37. On the nature of entrepreneurship and profit and loss see Herbener, Jeffrey, "The Role of Entrepreneurship in Desocialization," *The Review of Austrian Economics*, Vol. 6, No. 1, (1992) 79–93 (See especially 79–86); and Mises, *Human Action*, 286–97.

38. On the importance of market prices for economic calculation, see Mises, "Economic Calculation in the Socialist Commonwealth," (Auburn, Alabama: The Ludwig von Mises Institute, 1990); Mises, *Socialism*, (Indianapolis, Indiana: Liberty Classics, 1981), 95–130; and Mises, *Human Action*, 694–11.

development of the division of labor, the accumulation of capital, and successful entrepreneurship. Searching for a common condition that is necessary for all of the above to function, one finds that all require the institution of private property.

Because it is voluntary exchange that makes the development of the division of labor possible, we will benefit from the division of labor only if dwelling in a society with institutions supporting voluntary trade. We can only engage in exchange in an environment of private property. Therefore, in order to take advantage of the division of labor and benefit from the economic development that flows from it, members of society must be secure in their property. Likewise, for capitalists to have the incentive to accumulate capital, they must be secure in their property. If, for example, the state enforces confiscatory taxation, capital accumulation is hindered because taxes reduce net incomes, so capitalists have a smaller quantity of money available for savings and investment. Additionally, capitalists have less incentive to save and invest, because they are guaranteed a smaller return on their investment.

The entrepreneur's need for monetary market prices in order to calculate profit and loss also points to the necessity of private property for entrepreneurship. Only voluntary prices are manifestations of the subjective values of the buyers and sellers in society. Again, voluntary exchange requires private property. Without voluntary exchange, there can be neither money nor market prices. Without economic calculation, those directing the allocation of factors of production have no way to know how to allocate them wisely. Capital is consumed and standards of living fall.

A corollary of security of private property is security in general. For the division of labor to develop and extend, society must enjoy peace. As Mises says, "The market economy involves peaceful cooperation. It bursts asunder when the citizens turn into warriors, and instead of exchanging commodities and services, fight one another."[39] The division of labor is able to develop only because its participants expect lasting peace and the ability to exchange that goes along with such peace. Conflict destroys the division of labor, because it forces each group to consume only what it produces.

Private Property: A Moral Imperative

One stands amazed at God's glory when he meditates upon the fact that the social institution required for us to fulfill the cultural mandate is precisely the social institution mandated by God's moral law prohibiting murder,

---

39. Mises, *Human Action*, 817.

theft, and covetousness. It is not enough to know that private property will achieve a certain end, like economic prosperity. The chief end of man is to glorify God and enjoy Him forever. The fundamental question regarding social institutions is not are they useful, but are they right.

Historically, Christians have recognized that private property is a Christian social institution. While there are many warnings against greed, trusting riches, and the love of money, and exhortations to share with those less fortunate, nowhere is the possession of property condemned. In fact, the commandments against theft indicate that God's moral law requires private property. Early church fathers such as Clement of Alexandria (ca. 190–215 AD), Cyprian (200–250 AD) and Augustine (354–430 AD) endorsed private property and allowed for the possession of riches, while cautioning Christians not to become ensnared by it, but to use their property for the good of the community.[40] The towering theologian during the Christian Middle Ages, Thomas Aquinas, was a firm believer in the superiority of private property over communal property, basing his convictions on both natural and divine law.[41] Likewise, key figures of the Protestant Reformation such as John Calvin also argued for the legitimacy of private property. The Christian view of private property was commonplace in the writings of nineteenth century pastors and theologians Charles Hodge, Francis Wayland, and R. L. Dabney.[42] Christians throughout history have concluded that there is a divine right to private property because of the biblical commandments against murder, theft, and coveting that are applied both to private citizens and their rulers.

Belief, Culture, and Economic Development

Peace and private property, however, do not guarantee economic progress. They only make it possible. Because economic progress requires saving and capital accumulation, prosperity requires relatively low social time preferences. Consequently, cultural values formed by philosophic and religious beliefs are also very important. Cultures that are predisposed to highly value present consumption will not progress economically. On the other hand, historian David Landes identifies the stress seventeenth

---

40. On early church fathers' perspective on property see Rothbard, Murray, *Economic Thought Before Adam Smith*, (Cheltenham, UK: Edward Elgar, 1995), 32–36.

41. Ibid., 51–58.

42. Hodge, Charles, *Systematic Theology*, Volume III (Hendrickson Publishers), 421–37; Wayland, Francis *Elements of Moral Science*, (Boston: Gould and Lincoln, 1856), 229–36; and Dabney, R. L., *Systematic Theology*, (Edinburgh, Scotland: The Banner of Truth Trust, 2002), 414–18.

century Protestants placed on redeeming the time as a significant reason for the flourishing of economic development in Northern Europe.[43] The Protestant doctrine of the sanctification of work has also been cited as a source of a moral system suitable for the development of commercial capitalism.[44]

Cultural and moral values also affect the ease with which peace and private property are maintained. As market participants succumb to greed, they will be more likely to lobby for state granted privileges via market regulation, reducing the scope of private property. Increased likelihood of fraud and theft increases uncertainty and results in more resources directed away from producing goods and more toward protecting property. God told our first parents to be fruitful and multiply, fill the earth, subdue it and have dominion over every living creature. The only way to cultivate and fill the earth without descending into a barbaric struggle for survival is to take advantage of the social division of labor, capital accumulation and wise entrepreneurship. Allowing these sources of economic progress to flourish requires the security provided by peace and private property sustained by and combined with cultural values such as a forsaking of theft and low social time preferences.

Conclusion:

Fulfilling God's cultural and moral mandate requires the social institution of private property. Economic development necessitates economic freedom. We should not confuse economic freedom and the right to private property with political freedom. Even democracy, for example, is no panacea for economic development. Democracy is merely a human political institution. Like all human institutions, democracy can be used either for good or for evil. The experience of the United States shows us that democracy does not guarantee economic freedom. Our democratically elected politicians regularly aggress against the right of property. They preside over the nation's confiscatory tax system, its manipulation of the money supply, its labor regulations, price controls and all of its other interventions. In fact, as democracy has expanded throughout our history, the U.S. regulatory code has continually increased.

---

43. Landes, David S., *The Wealth and Poverty of Nations*, (New York: W. W. Norton & Company, 1999), 174–81.

44. Rosenberg, Nathan and L. E. Birdzell, Jr., *How the West Grew Rich*, (New York: Basic Books, Inc., 1986), 128–34.

This is not meant to be an argument against democracy, but only to point out that, from the perspective of fulfilling the cultural mandate, the important institution is private property and not free elections. To the extent that a society has political freedom, it should use that freedom to keep the peace and protect private property. Only real peace coupled with private property and the cultural values that sustain it will enable people to participate more ably in the fulfillment of the mandate God gave both their and our first parents in the beginning.

Shawn Ritenour is an Associate Professor of Economics at Grove City College and an adjunct Professor with the Von Mises Institute. He holds a BS from Northwestern College, and the PhD from Auburn University.

12

Leadership and Motivation

"But Jesus called them over and said, 'You know that the rulers of the Gentiles dominate them, and the men of high position exercise power over them. It must not be like that among you. On the contrary, whoever wants to become great among you must be your servant, and whoever wants to be first among you must be your slave; just as the Son of Man did not come to be served, but to serve, and to give His life a ransom for many."
—Matt. 20:25–28

"Give no offense to Jews or to Greeks or to the church of God,
just as I try to please everyone in everything I do,
not seeking my own advantage,
but that of many, that they may be saved."
—1 Cor. 10:32–33 ESV

"The hand of the diligent will rule,
but the lazy man will be put to forced labor."
—Prov. 12:24 NKJV

"If I had to go through the arrest again, I would do it. I live without regrets. I try to do the best I can with the present and hope for the best in whatever the future brings. The past takes care of itself."
—Rosa Parks

"Setting a goal is not the main thing. It is deciding
how you will go about achieving it and staying with that plan."
—Tom Landry

"Grace makes it possible not only for us to want to do what is right
but actually to do it not in our own strength but by the help
of our Deliverer, who at the resurrection will give us
that perfect peace which is the consequence of good will."
—Augustine

"No matter how badly we have failed,
we can always get up and begin again.
Our God is the God of new beginnings."
—Warren Wiersbe

"One of the most common mistakes people make
is trying to lead others before developing
relationships with them."
—John Maxwell

"People who are dried out within can often be, for a while,
the hardest workers. But they can also become the harshest critics
and the most negative teammates."
—Gordon MacDonald

Style, Power, and the Servant Leader

David Wesley Whitlock

UNDERSTANDING LEADERSHIP styles, power, and motivational theories is extremely advantageous for a manager. Some argue it is critical. Leadership style refers to the manner in which a person motivates (or at least attempts to motivate) others. Power refers to the ability of a person to influence the behavior of another. Motivation, from the Latin *motus*, means to propel or move forward. How a Christian leads and motivates has a profound influence beyond personal and organizational success. While believers are to have strong work ethics, working unto the Lord, their motivational bases, power bases and leadership styles can affect their personal witness and others' views of Christian ethics.

Four common leadership styles include: Autocratic, Benevolent Autocratic, Democratic, and Laissez Faire. Rather than thinking of these as independent styles, instead picture them on a line. Most people will fall somewhere nearer one of these styles: Autocratic—Benevolent Autocratic—Democratic—Laissez Faire.

Autocratic leadership refers to a dictatorial style. In this style, the leader declares or dictates an action and followers are expected to do as the leader commands, without question. Autocrats are likely to use coercion as a power base. The benevolent autocratic leadership is similar to the autocrat but with less reliance on sheer coercion. There may be more reasoning or explanation given, but the basic style of dictating an action and expected obedience is still present. Some refer to this is as the *friendly dictator* style of leadership.

Democratic leadership refers to a style that is participatory in nature. Gathering opinions and input from followers and democratic decision making are associated with this style of leadership. Sometimes this is referred to in business as participative management. Laissez Faire Leadership is basically *free reign* among a given group of people—democratic leadership at the extreme end of the spectrum. Some might argue that this is no leadership at all and, therefore, not truly a style of leadership but simply the absence of leadership.

Part II: A Matter of Worldview

The best method of leadership is often determined by the type of work being accomplished, the organizational culture, personalities, and time constraints. In the middle of a safety crisis, participatory leadership and decision making is not necessarily the *Christian* means of leadership style (regardless of many Evangelicals' predisposition toward *congregationalism* in terms of polity). In that situation, a take-charge leader is needed directing others with precision and command. However, in all things, the Christian should be humble and treat subordinates and followers with the greatest respect. Likewise, the authority, or power, upon which leadership is based, must be exercised with great respect and concern for subordinates.

To effectively lead, power must be present. While many people may have a negative connotation associated with the concept of power, it is nonetheless imperative. For those who cannot imagine the good and benevolent nature of power, just consider that the Almighty God is vested with all power; and Scripture is clear that God is all good, all the time. Power is the ability to influence the behavior of another person. French and Raven identified five power bases[1] on which leaders and managers typically base their ability to motivate others. Usually, more than one power base is evident in any given situation. Their bases included: coercion, reward, expert, referent, and legitimate power.

Coercive power is the ability to influence another's behavior based on fear of harm, retribution or punishment. Threatening to fire or harm someone if he or she does not accomplish some task is an example of coercive power. Reward power is the ability to influence someone based on the ability to give something wanted, needed or valued by the follower. The ability to give a raise, bonus or grant time off to a subordinate is an example of reward power.

Expert power refers to the ability to influence another's behavior based on someone's need for specific information, knowledge or expertise. Similar to reward power, if a person needs information for decision making that another person has, then the one with that information has the ability to influence his or her behavior. Referent power is based on the charisma or trust that followers have in the leader. Sometimes referred to as *blind faith*, this power base rests largely on the personality of the leader. Finally, legitimate power is based on tradition or position. A manager has the ability to influence his or her subordinates based on the fact that the organization has endowed that manager with certain responsibilities and authority.

---

1. French, J. R. P., Jr., & Raven, B. H. "The Bases of Social Power." In D. Cartwright et al., *Studies in Social Power*. Ann Arbor: Institute for Social Research, 1959, pp. 150–167.

Leadership and Motivation

So what is a Christian professional's response? How can one use power responsibly and ethically? How can one apply leadership styles in an effective and biblical way? Consider the servant leadership model. Servant leadership has become a vogue concept in recent years, with training seminars and workshops dedicated to teaching the servant leader model. Too often though, the concept is devoid of the teachings of the original servant leader, Jesus, particularly as described in Matthew. "But Jesus called them over and said, 'You know that the rulers of the Gentiles dominate them, and the men of high position exercise power over them. It must not be like that among you. On the contrary, whoever wants to become great among you must be your servant, and whoever wants to be first among you must be your slave; just as the Son of Man did not come to be served, but to serve, and to give His life a ransom for many'" (Matt. 20:25–28).

Jesus taught his disciples that desiring greatness wasn't evil, but encouraged them that to be great, they had to serve others. He inverted what the modern concept of leadership is in most management organizations. It flies in the face of what many professionals think. But just examine the results that Jesus got from his followers. They would follow him anywhere. They were motivated! They were changed. Devout Jewish zealots and tax collectors came together for a greater purpose. Jesus served them, met their needs and in turn, they found common ground and gave themselves to that higher purpose. They began to see themselves how Jesus saw them. His served them. He washed their feet. He even gave his life for them.

Requirements for servant leadership are not easy though. Servant leadership demands:

- Humility as opposed to pride;
- Unselfishness as opposed to self-centeredness;
- Putting others' needs ahead of your own;
- Commitment;
- Uncompromising integrity and standards;
- Primary greatness as opposed to secondary greatness.

Understanding primary greatness and secondary greatness is critical. Covey has popularized these concepts and describes them in his book, *Principle-Centered Leadership*. Many people—government leaders, business executives, and professionals—are perceived as great and yet, they seem to have no core—no guiding set of principles. Covey argues that primary greatness is not based on personality or charisma or popularity; that is secondary greatness.[2] The *cult of celebrity* is how so much of

---

2. Covey, Stephen R., *Principle-Centered Leadership*, Simon & Schuster, 1990, New York. p. 57–66

the world defines greatness. This is particularly seen with television and movie stars, but also with elected officials and powerful business leaders. Sadly, it is too often indicative of church leaders, pastors, evangelists and in contemporary Christian music. But primary greatness is achievement or accomplishment based on (as Covey has written), "genuineness," and "goodness of character."[3]

Primary greatness is what leads the leader and motivates the motivator to seek to be a servant leader. And the outcomes of servant leadership are tremendous. In fact, when one implements and practices true servant leadership, the outcomes observed will mirror those that were reflected in the lives of Christ's followers. The outcomes of servant leadership include:

- Changed lives—followers see life as having purpose and meaning;
- Followers who recognize the difference between primary greatness and secondary greatness and pursue the first;
- Followers who see themselves through their leader's eyes and realize their full potential.

The difference is to take the world's concept of management and leadership (having everyone below you at your beck and call and viewing them as people who are to serve you) and inverting that concept. Picture the models of management as a hierarchy from supervisory to middle management to executive-level management at the top. Now invert that in terms of who serves whom. The model Jesus provided adopts the view that you as a manager or leader are there to serve them, assist them, and be a source of assistance and encouragement. Supervisors ought to view their role as meeting the needs of subordinates and considering others before themselves.

David Wesley Whitlock serves as the Associate Provost, Dean of the College of Business and Computer Science, and Professor of Business Administration at Southwest Baptist University. He earned his BS and MBA from Southeastern Oklahoma State University, and the PhD from the University of Oklahoma.

3. Ibid.

Free to Serve

Tom D. Stevens

The Dead Sea, located between Jordan and Israel, is the lowest surface point on earth at 1,371 feet below sea level. It also happens to be one of the saltiest bodies of water with salt concentrations nearly eight times greater than the ocean. Although the density of the Dead Sea's saltwater provides a good flotation surface for fascinated tourists, the heavy concentrations of salt make it nearly impossible for aquatic life to survive. Yet, despite the absence of life in the Dead Sea, there are surprisingly over 150 sources of fresh water and aquatic life that feed into the sea. How is it then that a body of water with so many sources of life cannot sustain life? The answer is simple. The Dead Sea has no outlets. When the fresh water and aquatic life enter the Dead Sea the water becomes stagnant, salt forms, and the aquatic life dies.

I am convinced that we as Christians often suffer from the Dead Sea effect in our lives because we lack a critical outlet for our faith—service. Immersed within a consumption-driven society, we are deceived into believing that the freedom Jesus Christ has granted us is purely for our own good and enjoyment. Have you ever considered, however, the possibility that we have been freed from the law of sin so that we might serve one another? This is the very message with which the Apostle Paul encouraged the Galatians, writing, "For you were called to freedom, brethren; only do not turn your freedom into an opportunity for the flesh, but through love serve one another" (Gal. 5:13 NASB). Are you using your freedom to serve?

As you seek to answer this question, it is helpful to reflect on the example of service displayed by our Lord and Savior, Jesus Christ. In Philippians, Paul writes of Christ and his human incarnation that he "made himself nothing, taking the very nature of a servant, being made in human likeness" (Phil. 2:7 NIV). What an incredible statement. Rather, what an incredible act by our Savior! Most of us spend our entire lives trying to become something or somebody. We seek to gain status, authority or wealth in hopes of building a lasting legacy. Yet, Christ, having all of the privileges of His Father, in an instant chose to lay aside his heavenly privileges and become nothing so that you and I might have everything. I suppose we could assert that Christ's act of humility sets a standard for service far beyond what we are capable of achieving. However, that would require us to ignore Paul's introductory words to this passage in which he urges, "Your attitude *should be the same* as that of Christ Jesus" (Phil. 2:5 NIV italics added).

By no means is it easy to lay aside our privileges for the sake of others. During my studies at seminary, I worked as a membership services coordinator at a YMCA located in a relatively affluent neighborhood. The very nature of my job was to serve the YMCA members, even on their less cordial days. I realized very soon that for most people my education, international experiences, and other résumé builders I identified myself with did not really matter. To most members, I was simply the guy who was responsible if there were not enough towels in the workout room; or, the guy to blame if the televisions were set to the wrong channel; or worse yet, the guy to call when the toilet was plugged in the bathroom. I recall thinking once as toilet water squirted onto my slacks from beneath the plunger, "this must be what the word *services* in *membership services* truly means." I eventually discovered a variety of reasons the word service was in my job title, many more of them equally unpleasant.

Although you may not be in a service profession, and your job title may not include the word *services*, as Christians we have all been called into the business of service. And despite what we might think from time to time, not a single one of us is overqualified for the job. In fact, the job has very little to do with qualifications and everything to do with attitude. In his letter to the Romans, Paul sought to remind the Christian community of this principle, writing, "Do not conform any longer to the pattern of this world, but be transformed by the renewing of your mind. Then you will be able to test and approve what God's will is—His good, pleasing and perfect will. For by the grace given me I say to every one of you: Do not think of yourself more highly than you ought, but rather think of yourself with sober judgment, in accordance with the measure of faith God has given you" (Rom. 12:2–3 NIV).

Thinking too highly of one's self was a problem common even among Jesus' disciples. On one occasion, after watching and hearing his disciples argue about position and power, Christ responded saying, "Not so with you. Instead, whoever wants to become great among you must be your servant, and whoever wants to be first must be your slave—just as the Son of Man did not come to be served, but to serve, and to give his life as a ransom for many" (Matt. 20:26–28 NIV). I love the first four words of these verses, "Not so with you." This could be the tagline for most of Jesus' teachings. The disciples, confronted by the same basic worldly influences we face today, were constantly comparing themselves to those around them. Yet, Jesus was continually reminding them that the principles of the Kingdom of God are in stark contrast to the principles of this world. The disciples were seeking greatness by being first, yet Jesus challenged them to seek greatness by being last.

Jesus' response to his disciples regarding power and position was not a declaration about what types of positions we should hold. In fact, some of the most sincere and servant-minded Christians I know hold rather prominent positions in their organizations. By no means is Jesus encouraging us to seek demotions in order to be real servants. If that was Jesus' message, it would be quite easy to achieve. Instead, Jesus' teaching is a statement about what our attitudes about ourselves and those around us should be regardless of the position we hold. As Jesus watched and heard his disciples argue over who would be the greatest among them, he recognized that their inward-focus was a paralyzing force that would prevent them from serving. Many of us today suffer from this same paralyzing force. Our inward-focus prevents us from living in the freedom we have been granted for the purpose of serving one another. So, how are you using your freedom?

In our quest to share Christ's servant attitude, it is important to recognize that the desire and ability to serve one another is not the natural crying of our hearts. This is a no-brainer for most of us. Perhaps this is why Paul wrote to the Galatians, "Through *love*, serve one another" (Gal. 5:13 NIV). But where does this love come from? Are we expected to magically conjure up this love so that we might then be motivated to serve? According to Paul, the love that enables us to serve is a fruit of the Spirit's work in our lives. As Paul asserted, "But the fruit of the Spirit is love, joy, peace, patience, kindness, goodness, faithfulness, gentleness, self-control; against such things there is no law" (Gal. 5:22–23 NIV). Not only has Christ freed us to serve one another, but he has also equipped us with the love, patience, kindness, goodness, and gentleness needed to truly serve one another. Yet, even though we are freed to serve and equipped to serve, the choice to serve is still a choice each one of us must make.

Perhaps the most spiritually dry period in my life was during seminary. I entered seminary, somewhat naively, with a variety of utopian expectations of what the experience would entail. Equipped with a passion to study and understand God's Word, I couldn't imagine a better place to spend two years of my life. Yet, within a few months, I found myself in a spiritual desert. Despite being fed weekly by some of the greatest biblical scholars and teachers in North America, I was unimpressed. So, I did what most of us do during such times. I devoted myself to my job, and I simply went through the motions of what was expected of me spiritually. How could this happen in such a spiritually rich environment?

At least part of the answer is found is Proverbs, which says, "He who is full loathes honey, but to the hungry even what is bitter tastes sweet" (Prov. 27:7 NIV). After only one semester of seminary, I was filled to the brim with sound Biblical teaching, to the point of loathing even the best sermon or devotion. However, the problem was not in my excessive consumption of such great teaching, but rather in my failure to use my training in service to others. Much like the Dead Sea, I had countless sources of life flowing into me; yet, failing to recognize the importance of service in my life, I had no outlets for my faith. Spiritually, I was stagnating and slowly dying inside. I was using the freedom granted me by Christ to serve myself rather than others. Yet, as I began to seek out opportunities at work, church, and throughout the community to serve, I once again began to experience the life which accompanies the freedom we have in Christ.

As the Apostle Paul wrote, "For you were called to freedom, brethren; only do not turn your freedom into an opportunity for the flesh, but through love serve one another" (Gal. 5:13 NASB). How are you using your freedom?

Tom D. Stevens is an Instructor of Economics at Southwest Baptist University. He holds a BS from Southwest Baptist University, a MTS from Dallas Theological Seminary, and an MBA from Southern Methodist University.

Motivation: A New Model

David Wesley Whitlock

MOTIVATION REFERS to moving others forward toward the goal or mission of the organization using appropriate power bases and leadership styles. There are a number of motivational theories, and most are based on defining the needs of others. Understanding the needs and wants of followers is critical for leaders applying motivational theory. The assumption is that once a follower's specific needs are determined, the leader can then theoretically motivate them by providing them the opportunity to have that specific need met. Four theories are outlined, from the most widely known and recognized theories of Abraham Maslow, Douglas McGregor, and David McClelland, to the lesser known Core Values Model.

Maslow's Hierarchy

Proposed by Abraham Maslow, this theory is built upon a hierarchical pyramid of five need levels: physical needs, safety and security needs, social needs, ego needs and self-actualization needs. Maslow (1908–1970) was a proponent of humanistic psychology and central to his theory was the premise that individuals would be motivated by the lower level needs first and once a level was met, the person would move to the next level.

Physical needs refer to the need for air, food and water for example. Safety and security needs generally refer to the need to have shelter and basic security in terms of protection. These two levels constitute the lower-level needs in Maslow's hierarchy. Social needs refer to the need to belong, to feel accepted and loved. Ego needs refer to a person's need to accept oneself while Self-Actualization needs refer to the need to achieve one's full potential. These three needs constitute Maslow's upper-level needs.

In theory, managers and leaders can apply Maslow by correctly determining what level need the follower is experiencing. An assumption of Maslow's theory is that a higher level need will not motivate as long as all of the needs below are not met. In other words, if a person is hungry, appealing to that person's social needs is futile. Furthermore, once a level was met, Maslow's theory assumes it is no longer effective for motivation. For instance, once someone is fed, providing more food as an incentive to the person is ineffective.

One problem with Maslow's theory in practice is the many exceptions to those assumptions. Consider those who fast from food and report what Maslow would have termed as self-actualization experiences. How could they meet the highest level of need in his hierarchy by literally depriving themselves of the lower level needs? Another problem with the hierarchy of needs theory is the assumption that the needs are *levels* and that a satisfied need no longer motivates. When a husband and wife go out to dinner for example, need levels including physical, social, and even ego needs may be fulfilled simultaneously.

Douglas McGregor's Theory X and Theory Y

Douglas McGregor (1906–1964) proposed two general leadership or management styles. His theory is largely based on Maslow's work. His theory may be thought of as two ends of a continuum. At one end is the Theory X manager who views subordinates as basically lazy and unmotivated and in need of constant supervision. This manager assumes subordinates must be motivated by the carrot and stick method. At the other end of the continuum is the Theory Y manager who views subordinates as basically self-motivated and willing to take on responsibilities and tasks if given the freedom and opportunity to do so. Most fall somewhere in between these two extremes, leaning more toward one style or the other.

David McClelland's Motivation Needs

David McClelland (1917–1998) was particularly interested in employees whom he termed *achievement motivated*. He believed that achievement motivated individuals are generally the ones who make things happen and get results. In his theory, he identified three categories of needs. The need for achievement is defined as the attainment of realistic but challenging goals and advancement in the job. There is a strong need for feedback as to achievement and progress, and a need for a sense of accomplishment.

The need for power and authority is defined as the need to be influential, effective and make an impact. There is a strong need to lead and for the person's ideas to prevail. There is also motivation toward increasing his or her personal status and prestige. The third need is for affiliation, defined as the need for friendly relationships. There is motivation toward interaction with others people and a need to be liked and held in popular regard. Such people are referred to as *team players*.

Core Values Model

The Core Values Model (CVM) of motivation does not assume levels or a hierarchy of needs. It generalizes three broad areas of needs as opposed to levels: physical, social, and psychological. In terms of definitions, physical needs refer to the need for sleep, food, and water. Social needs refer to the need to affiliate or belong, to be accepted. Psychological needs generally coincide with the need for knowing and understanding oneself for a positive self concept and identity. It is tied to one's worldview. The CVM does not assume that one need must be met before other needs can be used for motivation. In fact, the CVM assumes that all three areas of needs can simultaneously motivate. The theory does recognize however, that at any given time, one need area may indeed be more dominant than the other two.

While Maslow's theory focuses largely on the object of motivation, McGregor focuses primarily on the leader or manager, and McClelland's theory focuses on the three driving motivators for human behavior, neither they nor others seem to adequately or seriously consider a person's core values—their spirituality. This is also true of most other motivational theories. And this, as any student of world religions will attest, is a critical component to understanding how to effectively motivate another person.

Therefore, central to the CVM approach to motivation and needs, is a person's core values, their spiritual base. Depending on these core values, a person will respond differently to any given stimulus. Correctly diagnosing the need area is insufficient; one must also understand what is at the

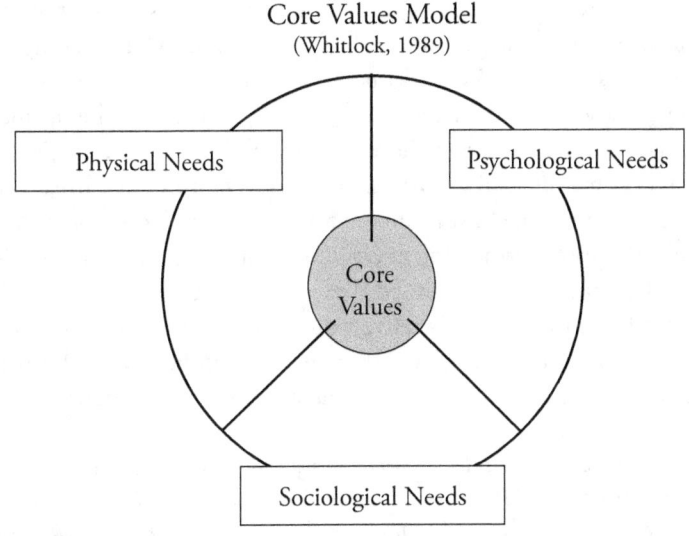

Core Values Model
(Whitlock, 1989)

person's core in order to effectively provide a truly motivational purpose or incentive to that person.

For example, a person may be correctly diagnosed as having a strong need for socialization. But without understanding that the person may have strong convictions on drinking due to her religion for example, a leader or manager may commit a faux pas by inviting him or her to a bar after work. The correct determination of need area is useless without considering the core values of the individual. Whatever the need a person may experience, that need is going to be related to the person's core belief system. In many ways the core values a person has can be considered a need itself as the core values are intrinsically linked with all other needs, wants, and desires of an individual, and failure to identify those core values and belief systems by which a person lives can negate any motivational effort.

These core values, regardless of whether someone is a person of faith or not manifest themselves, even if only through the conscience. The Word explains that the requirements of God's law are written on the hearts of men—even Gentiles—with their consciences and thoughts accusing and defending them. "For it is not those who hear the law who are righteous in God's sight, but it is those who obey the law who will be declared righteous. (Indeed, when Gentiles, who do not have the law, do by nature things required by the law, they are a law for themselves, even though they do not have the law, since they show that the requirements of the law are written on their hearts, their consciences also bearing witness, and their thoughts now accusing, now even defending them)" (Rom. 2:13–15).

Of interest to the theologian and evangelist perhaps, is the transformation of these core values upon a person's conversion to Christianity and their professions of faith. As God makes them new creations, these core values might be described in terms of the unspiritual man being made spiritual. As the spirit of a new believer is made alive in Christ, the person's core values become those of Christ. As the person matures in Christ, these core values become more and more conformed by the Holy Spirit to the very mind of Christ, permeating every action, attitude, and area of one's life. Regardless, these core values, be they the conscience of an the unbelieving Gentile, or the spiritually alive values and ministry of God's Spirit in the life of a Christian, will have tremendous significance on both the one who is attempting to motivate and the one being motivated.

David Wesley Whitlock serves as the Associate Provost, Dean of the College of Business and Computer Science, and Professor of Business Administration at Southwest Baptist University. He earned his BS and MBA from Southeastern Oklahoma State University, and the PhD from the University of Oklahoma.

Part III
A Matter of Faith

Putting It into Practice

- The Necessity of a Biblical Christian Worldview
- A Life of Faith
- Epilogue: A Challenge

13

Putting It into Practice

"At that time Abimelech, with Phicol the commander of his army, said to Abraham, "God is with you in everything you do. Now swear to me here by God that you will not break an agreement with me or with my children and descendants. As I have kept faith with you, so you will keep faith with me and with the country where you are a resident alien.' And Abraham said, 'I swear [it].'"
—Gen. 21:22–24

"Now therefore fear the LORD, and serve him in sincerity and in truth: and put away the gods which your fathers served on the other side of the flood, and in Egypt; and serve ye the LORD. And if it seem evil unto you to serve the LORD, choose you this day whom ye will serve; whether the gods which your fathers served that were on the other side of the flood, or the gods of the Amorites, in whose land ye dwell: but as for me and my house, we will serve the LORD."
—Josh. 24:14–15 NKJV

"And now, O Israel, what does the LORD your God ask of you but to fear the LORD your God, to walk in all his ways, to love him, to serve the LORD your God with all your heart and with all your soul"
—Deut. 10:12 NIV

The Necessity of a Biblical Christian Worldview

Gordon Dutile

PETER INSTRUCTS US: "But in your hearts set apart Christ as Lord. Always be prepared to give an answer to everyone who asks you to give the reason for the hope that you have. But do this with gentleness and respect" (1 Pet. 3:15 NIV). The word translated *answer* by the NIV literally means "a verbal defense." It is the Greek word from which we get our words apology and apologist. How are we believers going to be able to verbally defend our faith if we do not know what we believe and why we believe it? It is not enough to say that we are Christians. We must demonstrate by word and deed that our faith in Christ drives everything we do.

The more I observe our culture and its spiritual climate, the more I am convicted that the Christian community must equip its members with a solid and sound biblical worldview. What do we mean when we speak of a worldview? It is the framework of life into which everything fits. It is the filter through which every thought, philosophy, and action must pass. Robert A. Harris says,

> One way to understand the idea of a worldview is to say that it's a personal theory of everything. In other words, a worldview is a comprehensive and unifying way of looking at all of life, a means of bringing coherent meaning to one's experiences, thoughts, feelings and so on. Worldviews must be personally chosen and worked out, and they grow and develop as we learn and gain more knowledge and experience. A worldview includes values, beliefs, commitments, and, attitudes, together with biases and prejudices.[1]

Far too many Christians, whether knowingly or unknowingly, have adopted a two-sphere approach to life. Things that have to do with their relationship with God through Christ fall into the arena of faith; but the things that have to do with the physical, everyday world fall into the arena

---

1. Robert A. Harris, *The Integration of Faith and Learning: A Worldview Approach* (Eugene, OR: Cascade Books, 2004), p. 77.

of that which can be proven by experimentation and empirical data. They act as if the two spheres should not interact, and that to allow them to do so results in some kind of false union, an unholy alliance. That is why some can claim to be Christian and yet function in a worldly setting as though Christ had nothing to do with their actions. From the biblical perspective, not to integrate them is a false dichotomy that leaves the Lord out of a portion of life. The statement, "Jesus is either Lord of all or not Lord at all," comes to mind. A truly biblical Christian worldview sees the totality of life through the lens of a personal relationship with Jesus the Christ.

This worldview integrates three fundamental issues: (1) Creation—How did I get here? (2) The fall—Why am I like I am? (3) Redemption—What can be done about my condition?[2] Every Christian must come to the settled conviction that "In the beginning God created the heavens and the earth" (Gen. 1:1 NIV). The writer of Hebrews states, "By faith we understand that the worlds were prepared by the word of God, so that what is seen was not made out of things which are visible" (Heb. 11:3 NASB). A lot of discussion may occur about how God did it and what kind of time frame it involved. But for the Christian, there can be no question as to who did it.

People from various persuasions have offered theories and explanations about why wrong exists in the human arena. The Bible makes it clear. The first humans chose to do it their way instead of God's; they said my will, not Your will. That choice determined that all of humanity as offspring of the first Adam would be sinners. The universality of sin is proclaimed in both the Old and New Testaments. "When they sin against you—for there is no one who does not sin—" (1 Kings 8:46a NIV). "Everyone has turned away, they have together become corrupt; there is no one who does good, not even one" (Psa. 130:3 NIV). "For all have sinned and fall short of the glory of God" (Rom. 3:23 NIV). "But the Scripture declares that the whole world is a prisoner of sin, . . ." (Gal. 3:22a NIV). As a result of this rebellion, humanity does not seek God. Instead we hide from God, as Adam and Eve did. The psalmist says, "The Lord has looked down from heaven upon the sons of men, to see if there are any who understand, who seek after God. They have all turned aside; together they have become corrupt; there is no one who does good, not even one" (Ps. 14:2-3 NASB).

---

2. For an in-depth discussion of these, see Nancy Pearcey, *Total Truth: Liberating Christianity from Its Cultural Captivity* (Wheaton, IL: Crossway Books, 2004), pp. 82-95. Also, Cornelius Plantinga Jr., *Engaging God's World: A Christian Vision of Faith, Learning, and Living* (Grand Rapids, MI: Wm. B. Eerdmans, 2002), pp. 17-100.

Left to himself a human is in an inescapable predicament. Paul's description of this difficult plight says, "And you were dead in your trespasses and sins, in which you formerly walked according to the course of this world, according to the prince of the power of the air, of the spirit that is now working in the sons of disobedience. Among them we too all formerly lived in the lusts of our flesh, indulging the desires of the flesh and of the mind, and were by nature children of wrath, even as the rest" (Eph. 2:1-3 NASB).

Paul makes it clear that left alone a person is hopelessly doomed. We can be grateful that the story does not end there. The apostle continues, "*But God* (emphasis mine), being rich in mercy, because of His great love with which He loved us, even when we were dead in our transgressions, made us alive together with Christ (by grace you have been saved), and raised us up with Him, and seated us with Him in the heavenly *places*, in Christ Jesus, in order that in the ages to come He might show the surpassing riches of His grace in kindness toward us in Christ Jesus" (Eph. 2:4-7 NASB).

Every other worldview has man achieving his deliverance by his own effort. Christianity reveals that redemption is accomplished by the intervention of God. Notice in the passages from Ephesians that when the human is the subject of the action, there is spiritual death and damnation. When God is the subject of the action, there is life and deliverance. In the Garden of Eden, the first Adam said no to God's will and yes to self, and plunged his offspring into sin. Throughout Jesus' life on earth and in the Garden of Gethsemane, the second Adam said yes to God's will and no to self, and provided humanity an escape from condemnation.

It is through this three-pronged filter that the Christian must view life. The believer must not compartmentalize life, or segment it. Everything he or she does is to be done to honor God. "So whether you eat or drink or whatever you do, do it all for the glory of God" (1 Cor. 10:31 NIV). It is imperative that Christians develop a strong biblical worldview that impacts the entirety of life, including their academic, professional, recreational, and personal lives. Dr. David Dockery, in the introduction to *Shaping a Christian Worldview*, says,

> Christian worldview is not just one's personal faith expression, not just a theory. It is an all-consuming way of life, applicable to all spheres of life. . . . A Christian worldview is not built on two types of truth (religious and philosophical or scientific) but on a universal principle and all-embracing system that shapes religion, natural and social sciences, law, history, health care, the arts, the humanities, and all disciplines of study with application for all of life.[3]

3. David S. Dockery and Gregory Alan Thornbury, ed., *Shaping a Christian Worldview:*

Part III: A Matter of Faith

Each Christian is to live life in a way that the Lordship of Christ is evident. The lost world needs to recognize that believers have a hope that is beyond this world and age. Then they will inquire as to the reason for that hope. It is essential that at that moment the Christian be able to give a verbal defense with gentleness and respect. May we live by Paul's admonition: "For though we live in the world, we do not wage war as the world does. The weapons we fight with are not the weapons of the world. On the contrary, they have divine power to demolish arguments and every pretension that sets itself up against the knowledge of God, and we take captive every thought to make it obedient to Christ" (2 Cor. 10:3–5).

Gordon Dutile is the Provost at Southwest Baptist University where he also served for many years as a professor of Greek. He holds a BS from Louisiana Tech University, and the MDiv and PhD from Southwestern Baptist Theological Seminary.

The Foundations of Christian Higher Education (Nashville, TN: Broadman and Holman, 2002), p. 2.

A Life of Faith: Lessons from Joseph

David Wesley Whitlock

From the very beginning, Genesis speaks of divine design. In the beginning God created. In the beginning the great I Am created order from chaos. In the beginning God separated. God the Father, Son, and Spirit distinguished; He distinguished between light and dark, day and night, waters above and waters below. In the beginning the Heavenly Father called forth His crowning achievement, man and woman, made in His very own image. God's design for Adam and Eve began with a call to work, to have dominion. Within the first few chapters of Genesis, we read of the unique design God has for His children, beginning with Adam and Eve's obligations to each other. In the beginning chapters of Genesis, we read of Adam and Eve's rebellion against God and discover the awful truth of our own sin.

Yet even within the first three chapters of this book of beginnings, we discover that God's grand design included a future and a hope for Adam and Eve and all of us who with the whole of creation fell under the curse of sin and death. For even in the midst of their rebellion, God began pointing them toward a future Deliverer. Even after they found themselves separated from their Father-Creator, God promised that the Seed of Eve—in other words a son who would someday be born as a descendant—would be revealed and set things right. God began to reveal His plan for the Messiah who is Jesus Christ, the Word become flesh. And so even then, they began to live by faith in the promised Seed, the Messiah who would redeem them. In the beginning was divine design.

The first verses of Genesis begin with spectacular glory and splendor, and when God creates His universe He pronounces it good. And it was. Perfection. That's His standard. Genesis opens with design and precision and order and life—abundant life, thrilling life, life unhindered by evil, sin, and deceit. So in some ways, the end of Genesis is quite an indictment on those descended from Adam and Eve, and who were born in the marred and sin scarred image of God's first children. For the last chapter in Genesis begins and ends with death—first Jacob's and then Joseph's. The deaths of Jacob and Joseph bring to an end the story of the first three patriarchs of God's story, Abraham, Isaac, and Jacob, and it brings to an end the story of this man of faith named Joseph. But like the first few chapters of Genesis, this last chapter presents a wonderful truth, even placed between the two accounts of Jacob and Joseph dying. The last few paragraphs in the book (Gen. 50:1–26), speak of God's divine design—His divine design for our separation, our calling, and His divine design for future.

The chapter begins with the death of Israel and demonstrates the distinction between the family of Jacob and others, the separation that existed between those who belong to God and the world. The chapter begins with the great preparation and funeral procession that accompanied his body to his burial place. Some historians suggest that it was common for priests to carry out the practiced art of embalming and preparing the body for burial. Joseph's wife was the daughter of such a priest. Though perhaps not too much should be made of it, Joseph does not call these priests to prepare his father's body for burial, but instead commands his servants who were physicians trained in the medical arts to prepare Israel's body. If there was a distinction to be made between the priests and physicians, it was clearly because Israel was different; he, his family and the nation that would be thereafter called by his name were unique unto God, separate.

Following a forty-day embalming period, which was the practice for the Egyptians, a great funeral that lasted seventy days was set apart in which all of Israel's family and even the Egyptians mourned this great man of God. Whether the seventy days (a number that the Hebrews would recognize as perfection) included the forty days of embalming is not as significant as the fact that even the pagan unbelieving Egyptians were driven to recognize Israel's unique relationship with God. And that was recognized largely through the office and ministry of their prince, Joseph. A lengthy time of mourning by the whole nation marked Israel's death. When the days of mourning were complete, with Pharaoh's permission, Joseph set out on a journey to take the body of his father back to Canaan to be buried, just as his father had made him promise.

Quite a procession was seen leaving Egypt; in many ways, it was a foreshadowing of the mighty nation of Israel leaving Egypt, led by Moses several hundred years later. The contingent consisted of a host of Pharaoh's servants and the elders of his household and all the elders of Egypt plus Joseph and his entire household, Joseph's brothers, and all of Jacob's household. Except for children, wives, and their livestock that were left in Goshen, they all set out on horses and chariots in a royal funeral that verse nine states was a very impressive procession. It ended at the threshing floor of Atad, which is across the Jordan from Canaan. For seven days at the threshing floor of Atad on the east side of Jordan, the large delegation wept so loudly that the Canaanite inhabitants saw and heard it and were so impressed by the mourning Egyptians, that they renamed the place, Abel-mizraim, which some translate as the "mourning of Egypt."

In the next two verses though, there is quite a distinction made. Clearly in the preceding verses, the delegation consisted of both Egyptians and Hebrews. But suddenly, following the seven-day mourning period on the east side of Jordan, we read that Jacob's sons carried the body to the land of Canaan and buried him in the cave at Machpelah in the field near Mamre. This is the place in the Promised Land, which Abraham had years before purchased as a burial site, and where Abraham and Sarah were buried with Isaac and Rebekah, and where Leah was buried also. It appears then that this family of faith was separated from the unbelieving Egyptians as they crossed Jordan into Canaan.

The lesson is this. God's people are different. There is a unique design that God has placed upon the lives of those of us who belong to Him that separates us from the world around us. We are His own and His design for us to be holy, meaning distinct—different. "As obedient children do not be conformed to the desires of your former ignorance but as the One who called you is holy you also are to be holy in all your conduct; for it is written, Be holy because I am holy" (1 Pet. 1:14). "Do not be conformed to this age but be transformed by the renewing of your mind so that you may discern what is the good, pleasing and perfect will of God" (Rom. 12:2). Don't be like the unbelieving world around you. Don't think like the unbelieving world around you. Don't behave like the unbelieving world around you. You're one of God's children. You're different. You're distinct. You're separate. He is holy. You be holy.

I can hear the objections. I can hear the demand that Christians, therefore, withdraw from the world to the point of having no contact at all with the unbelieving world around us. But it is clear that there is also a call of God on our lives to carry out the divine design that He has given us, to fulfill the responsibilities God has placed upon us—be it our calling as parents, our vocational calling, or our calling as a royal priesthood. As Adam and Eve were called to work in the Garden, so too are we called to particular vocations where we are to faithfully serve God.

Joseph conveyed to Pharaoh that he had given his oath to his father to bury him in the family tomb in Canaan. In the fifth verse, he asked, "[L]et me go and bury my father." Then he made an oath to Pharaoh, "Then I will return" (Gen. 50:5). Let me... but I'll return. Joseph recognized that God's divine design had placed him in Egypt and that his responsibilities among the Egyptians were not complete. He had been called by God as the prince of Egypt. He had been called by God to be ruler, a manager. God's call on Joseph's life was as a husband to his wife in Egypt; it was as a father to Manasseh and Ephraim in Egypt. It was as a minister to Pharaoh in his vocation. It was as a provider and protector of his brothers and family in Goshen of Egypt.

Though we will return to this later, this call on the believer's life is demonstrated through Joseph's response to his brothers who appeal for his mercy on behalf of their father and on behalf of their shared faith in God with Joseph. Fearing retribution from Joseph, they repeat their father's plea for Joseph's mercy on their part. They demonstrate their repentance once again and their fear breaks the heart of Joseph. Joseph weeps and responds with more grace and mercy. "Am I in the place of God," he asked them. "Don't be afraid, I will take care of you and your little ones" (Gen. 50:19–21). He comforted them. He spoke kindly to them. Joseph's call extended to his place as a minister to his family, and he gives an oath to provide for them and assures them of his forgiveness. The design of God for their separation was not an invitation to ignore God's divine design for their calling to be examples and ministers of His glory and message. They had work to do. They had ministry to perform. They had testimony to be given and lives of faith to be demonstrated to an unbelieving world around them.

One of the most incredible prayers Jesus ever uttered was one in which He looked up to heaven and began praying for Himself and then for His followers. He prayed, "Father, the hour has come. Glorify Your Son so that the Son may glorify You . . . I have glorified You on the earth by completing the work You gave Me to do. Now Father glorify Me in Your presence with that glory I had with You before the world existed. I have revealed Your name to the men You gave Me from the world. They were Yours, You gave them to Me and they have kept Your word. . . I pray for them. I am not praying for the world but for those You have given Me because they are Yours. . . I am not praying that You take them out of the world but that You protect them from the evil one. They are not of the world as I am not of the world. . . . As you sent Me into the world I also have sent them into the world" (John 17:1, 4–6, 9, 15–16, 18).

The Father sent the Son who was distinct and separate and holy into the world. The Son sends us into the world. He prays not for us to be removed from the world but to be separate and holy in the world, ministering and fulfilling His call on our lives. While we are not to be conformed to the world around us, we are nonetheless called by God to be ministers of His glory, His message, His Good News. We are called to work, called to minister, called to testify, and called to demonstrate faith to an unbelieving world around us.

Finally, there is revealed in these last verses of Genesis, the truth that God has a divine design for the future. As stated earlier, the funeral of old Israel foreshadowed a future for the Israelites. In the very next book of the Bible, following hundreds of years in Egypt, including years of oppression, the Israelites would one day march again out of Egypt with great pomp and circumstance. And once again, the rest of the world would witness it and wonder in awe at such a great exodus. God had a design for the future of this little family, a future that would include their becoming a mighty nation that would one day inhabit Canaan and one day include bringing to the world the Savior. Jacob knew it, believed it, had faith that it was to be. So did Joseph. He knew it, believed it, and demonstrated his faith that it would happen.

As much as any person in the Bible, Joseph demonstrates what a life of faith looks like. His faith is shown in his actions as a slave, in his obedience to purity and resistance to temptation, in his ministry as a prisoner, in his steadfast convictions that God's promise to him would someday be fulfilled no matter what the circumstances seemed. His faith is shown in his work ethic and his consistency in fulfilling his assignments and responsibilities. His name is recorded alongside Abel, Enoch, Noah, Abraham, Sarah, Isaac, Jacob, Moses, Rahab, and the others listed in Hebrews 11, the famed *heroes of the faith* chapter. Among all of the demonstrations of his great faith that could have been recorded there for Joseph, do you know what God chose to reveal as the tremendous sign of Joseph's faith? "By faith Joseph, as he was nearing the end of his life, mentioned the exodus of the sons of Israel and gave instructions concerning his bones" (Heb. 11:22). His faith was demonstrated not in the actions he had demonstrated and could have pointed to at the end of his life. In other words, Joseph's faith was not in what he had seen but what he had yet to see. His faith was demonstrated in his firm conviction of what God would do in the future; it was in what he still yet could not see.

Even Joseph's own death at the age of 110, which ends the book, reveals that he was embalmed and placed in a coffin in Egypt but not buried. Wherever that coffin had been stored, it would have been pointed to for hundreds of years as God's people of faith would say, "See that coffin? It's the bones of Joseph and it will be buried one day in the Promised Land. For one day He will establish us there and we will be His own people, His own nation. One day, we'll leave this place for a place God has prepared for us."

God had a future and a hope for them, and it is demonstrated in Joseph's own burial instructions. Joseph lived a long and full life and saw his own children, grand-children, great grandchildren and by some interpretations, I am convinced that verse 23 suggests Joseph witnessed the births of his great, great grandchildren. In verses 24 and 25, we read the last words recorded by this man of faith. He called his brothers, those who were still yet alive and presumably the sons of his brothers who had died, and spoke to them. "I am about to die but God will certainly come to your aid and bring you out from this land to the land He promised Abraham, Isaac, and Jacob" (Gen. 50:24–25). He made them give him an oath that one day in the future when God visits them, comes to their rescue and delivers them, that they should take his bones from Egypt to the Promised Land. What a sign of faith!

The encounter of Joseph and his brothers following the burial of Israel is touching for many reasons. Their repentance and request of Joseph for mercy demonstrates a truth about sin. It gnaws on you. It haunts you. It brings fear and dread. Sin and disobedience eat away at you as it did these brothers. But Joseph's response is one of my favorite passages in the Bible. In verses 19-22 are recorded some of the most comforting passages in the Bible. After they fell at his feet and pledged themselves as slaves to him we read, "But Joseph said to them, 'Don't be afraid. Am I in the place of God? You planned evil against me; God planned it for good to bring out the present result—the survival of many people. Therefore, don't be afraid. I will take care of you and your little ones.' And he comforted them and spoke kindly to them" (Gen. 50:19–22).

Perhaps no other passage in God's Word speaks so eloquently of God's sovereignty. Look at the world and you see so much sin and so much hurt and so much fear and so much oppression and so much war and so much pain and so much hunger and so much suffering, and it is absolutely overwhelming. Yet, what has been meant for evil, God will turn for good. He works all things together for good for those who love Him and are called according to His purpose. He has a future and a hope for those who are called by His name. God will get glory out of all of this, somehow, some way.

Our future is secure. God is working all things together for good for those who believe in Messiah, Jesus. The Messiah who was promised in the beginning, did indeed come. He offered Himself as a sacrifice for our sin. He was crucified, buried, and raised from the dead on the third day. For those who fall at his feet and repent, who plead for His mercy and His grace, who confess that their sin crucified Him, their evil caused Him to suffer and die, He says, "Don't be afraid. I am. You planned evil against me; the Father planned it for good to bring out the present result—your salvation, your eternal life. Therefore, don't be afraid. I will take care of you." Jesus forgives completely. He gives eternal life and promises to someday deliver us from this world into a new world. Our faith is a faith in our future. Our hope is heaven, a place we are as convinced of as Jacob and Joseph were of the Promised Land.

Genesis ends with a world radically changed from the perfection pictured in the beginning. Still yet, there is a great hope, a certain future and the assurance of divine design. There is, even in the closing chapters of Genesis, a great charge for those who, day in and day out, fulfill their assignments and responsibilities. Be faithful. Serve even when others don't support you. Be faithful. Do your best in spite of the circumstances. Be faithful. Trust that God is always in charge no matter the situation and that He is working all things together for good for those who love Him and are called according to His purpose.

David Wesley Whitlock serves as the Associate Provost, Dean of the College of Business and Computer Science, and Professor of Business Administration at Southwest Baptist University. He holds the BS and MBA from Southeastern Oklahoma State University, and the PhD from the University of Oklahoma.

Epilogue

A Challenge

OF COURSE, writers hope not just to be read, but to be heard. The hope of each contributor to this work is that you have been challenged to think (or rethink) each of the topics addressed. Whether it was a devotional that caused you to consider your own character traits or an essay that stirred you to reconsider your worldview, our hope is that you have come to the conclusion that as a Christian, God has placed (or will place) you in a unique position of influence. Others will watch you. They will observe whether or not your Christianity makes any difference in the way you conduct yourself professionally and personally. People are hungry to see consistency in the life of a believer. This is especially true, I am convinced, in the marketplace.

If you are a Christian, will you prayerfully consider the words penned in this book of devotions and essays? Will you commit to a life that is marked by integrity, service, respect, charity, faithfulness, truthfulness, humility and perseverance? Will you consider whether or not your own faith is so private and hidden that it has no impact or relevance to your life as a professional? Remember the words found in James: "Foolish man! Are you willing to learn that faith without works is useless?" (James 2:20 NKJV). Prayerfully consider how your worldview impacts the way you conduct yourself at work, at home, in private and when no one is watching. Put your faith into practice! Remember the concept of stewardship of experience. God desires to use everything you have experienced including your education, and work life.

For those who have yet to believe and place their faith in the person of Jesus Christ, there is this challenge. Consider the writings in this book and examine your own life in light of a biblical worldview. Each of the authors in this book has achieved personal and professional success and enjoyed many years of education and advanced degrees. Yet, at our core, each of us faces the same problem. We know deep down that there is a God and that we are separated from Him. Our challenge is that you would read the following brief explanation of being right with God. Our prayer is that you would open your mind to how God may speak to you.

Our Problem

God created us in His own image to have an abundant life. The first man and woman, Adam and Eve, were made perfect and lived without sin until they rebelled against God. Now, all of Adam's descendants, including you, live under the curse of death and sin. Everyone has deliberately chosen to disobey God. In our own sinful state no one is even able to seek after God. The result is our separation from God and the sentence of death and hell upon us.

As it is written, *"There is none who understands; there is none who seeks after God. They have all gone out of the way; they have together become unprofitable; There is none who does good, no not one"* (Rom. 3:10–12 NKJV). *"Now we know that whatever the law says, it says to those who are under the law, that every mouth may be stopped, and all the world may become guilty before God. Therefore by the deeds of the law no flesh will be justified in His sight, for by the law is the knowledge of sin"* (Rom. 3:19–20 NKJV). *For all have sinned and fall short of the glory of God"* (Rom. 3:23 NKJV). *For the wages of sin is death, but the gift of God is eternal life in Christ Jesus our Lord"* (Rom. 6:23 NKJV). Our situation is desperate. We are separated from God and incapable of doing anything about it. We have sinned and are under the curse of death and punishment.

God's Answer

Though we are deserving of punishment and judgment, God is merciful and loving. God provided an answer to our problem: Jesus the Christ, meaning the Messiah or Savior. Jesus lived a perfect life without any sin. He offered Himself as the sacrifice for our sin. Jesus took the punishment of death upon himself. He died on the cross and three days later rose from the dead, securing forgiveness and eternal life for all who surrender to Him and trust in Him alone. He paid the penalty for our sin. Discover the greatest joy known to man—knowing the God who created you. Are you humbled and grieved to learn of your sin? Do you want to be forgiven and made right with God?

"The Lord is merciful and gracious, slow to anger and plenteous in mercy" (Ps. 103:8 NKJV). *"For God so loved the world that He gave His only begotten Son, that whoever believes in Him should not perish but have everlasting*

life" (John 3:16 NKJV). *"But God demonstrates His own love for us in this: While we were still sinners, Christ died for us"* (Rom. 5:8 NKJV). *"And as it is appointed unto man once to die, and after this the judgment, so Christ was once offered to bear the sins of many; and unto them that look for him shall he appear the second time without sin unto salvation"* (Heb. 9:27 NKJV). Are you humbled and grieved to learn of your sin? Do you want to be forgiven and made right with God?

Our Response

We must confess and repent (turn away from our sins) and surrender our lives totally to Him. God commands you to repent and believe in the Lord Jesus. God even grants you the faith required to believe. True converts will have enduring evidence of their salvation and will love and fellowship with God's people in a local church. They will bear spiritual fruit, and they will endure unto the end as they watch and eagerly wait for the Lord to return as He promised.

"If you confess with your mouth the Lord Jesus and believe in your heart that God has raised Him from the dead, you will be saved. For whoever calls upon the name of the Lord will be saved" (Rom. 10:9, 13 NKJV). *"For it is by grace you have been saved, through faith and this is not of yourselves, it is the gift of God not by works, so that no one can boast"* (Eph. 2.8–9 NKJV). *"And let us consider one another in order to stir up love and good works, not forsaking the assembling of ourselves together, as is the manner of some, but exhorting one another, and so much the more as you see the Day approaching"* (Heb. 10:24–25 NKJV). *"But the fruit of the Spirit is love, joy, peace, longsuffering, kindness, goodness, faithfulness, gentleness, self-control"* (Gal. 5:22–23 NKJV). *"In My Father's house are many mansions; if it were not so, I would have told you. I go to prepare a place for you. And if I go and prepare a place for you, I will come again and receive you to Myself; that where I am, there you may be also. And where I go you know, and the way you know"* (John 14:2–4 NKJV).

Pray to God and confess your sins to Him. Turn from your sin and ask Him to forgive you. Place your faith in Jesus, His death on a cross in your place, and His resurrection from the dead. Surrender your will to Jesus and find a local church to help you in your Christian walk. As Ephesians 4:1 urges, walk worthy of the calling you have received.

DWW

Appendix

- Usury and Interest: A Christian Perspective

- Capital Rationing and the Fall

Usury and Interest:
A Christian Perspective

David Wesley Whitlock

The fifteenth Psalm outlines principles that should characterize the believer. These principles are specifically helpful for professionals who face many challenges and dilemmas throughout their careers. The Psalm describes the kind of person who dwells with the Lord and one of the prohibitions given is the charging of usury. Some translations simply refer to interest.

The principle taught in the Bible concerning interest seems predominately centered on not charging interest to *brothers* but rather giving to them what they need without interest. Deuteronomy states: "Do not charge your brother interest on money, food, or anything that may earn interest" (Deut. 23:19 NIV). Nehemiah was particularly incensed when it was discovered that the Jews were not abiding by this prohibition (See Neh. 5:7–11). In addition to Psalm 15:4–6 and the passages from Deuteronomy and Nehemiah, other references to this prohibition include: Exod. 22:25; Lev. 25:37; Ezek. 18:7–9; Ezek. 18:12–14; Ezek. 22:12.

However, the prohibition against interest does not seem to hold when dealing with those outside the family of faith. "You may charge a foreigner interest, but not a brother Israelite, so that the LORD your God may bless you in everything you put your hand to in the land you are entering to possess" (Deut. 23:20 NIV).

But even then, it appears that usury is prohibited. For example, "Do not mistreat an alien or oppress him, for you were aliens in Egypt" (Exod. 22:21 NIV). Usury is charging exorbitant interest rates above what is customary or reasonable. So even in dealing with *strangers* or *foreigners*, the Jews were commanded to be fair in charging interest on loans.

What principles are taught in the New Testament regarding interest on loans? Examine Matthew's gospel:

> Again, it will be like a man going on a journey, who called his servants and entrusted his property to them. To one he gave five

Appendix

talents of money, to another two talents, and to another one talent, each according to his ability. Then he went on his journey. The man who had received the five talents went at once and put his money to work and gained five more. So also, the one with the two talents gained two more. But the man who had received the one talent went off, dug a hole in the ground and hid his master's money.

After a long time the master of those servants returned and settled accounts with them. The man who had received the five talents brought the other five. "Master," he said, "you entrusted me with five talents. See, I have gained five more." His master replied, "Well done, good and faithful servant! You have been faithful with a few things; I will put you in charge of many things. Come and share your master's happiness!" The man with the two talents also came. "Master," he said, "you entrusted me with two talents; see, I have gained two more." His master replied, "Well done, good and faithful servant! You have been faithful with a few things; I will put you in charge of many things. Come and share your master's happiness!"

Then the man who had received the one talent came. "Master," he said, "I knew that you are a hard man, harvesting where you have not sown and gathering where you have not scattered seed. So I was afraid and went out and hid your talent in the ground. See, here is what belongs to you." His master replied, "You wicked, lazy servant! So you knew that I harvest where I have not sown and gather where I have not scattered seed? Well then, you should have put my money on deposit with the bankers, so that when I returned I would have received it back with interest. Take the talent from him and give it to the one who has the ten talents. For everyone who has will be given more and he will have an abundance. Whoever does not have, even what he has will be taken from him. And throw that worthless servant outside, into the darkness, where there will be weeping and gnashing of teeth." (Matt. 25:14–23 NIV)[1]

The New Testament does refer to the collection of interest on money deposited with a bank or lender. But are the parables in which this is mentioned meant to condone the practice? After all, the parables were not specifically about interest or usury. In Matthew 5:42, Jesus urges His followers to lend to whoever asks for a loan. Should the Christian refrain from charging interest? It would appear that while there are no direct commandments for believers, some guidelines are worth noting.

Neither lending nor borrowing is specifically condemned in the Bible. Jesus even taught His followers, "Give to the one who asks you, and don't

---

1. Also see Luke 19:11–27.

turn away from the one who wants to borrow from you" (Matt. 5:42 NIV) Furthermore, Christians may lend to anyone, Christians and non-Christians as seen in Luke: "And if you lend to those from whom you expect to receive, what credit is that to you? Even sinners lend to sinners to be repaid in full. But love your enemies, do [what is] good, and lend, expecting nothing in return. Then your reward will be great, and you will be sons of the Most High. For He is gracious to the ungrateful and evil" (Luke 6:34–35).

In the practice of lending, Christians should not charge interest on loans made to other Christians. This would keep with the general teaching of Scripture and is consistent with teachings in both the Old and New Testament. Furthermore, in the practice of lending, it can be argued that charging interest on a loan made to a non-believer is permissible, but that under no circumstance should the interest be outside of normal, accepted rates. Usury is prohibited in the practice of lending in all situations.

Finally, these principles are intended primarily for individual believers in their personal decision making. They may not directly apply to an institution such as a bank or mortgage company in which a person is employed and made responsible for granting loans. In such a case, the Christian is not making decisions to lend from his or her personal supply, but on behalf of a corporation; he or she is not making personal loans, but investing the money of others. As such, there would appear to be no prohibition against Christians working at a bank to make loans consistent with the rules and regulations set forth by their employer, state and professional codes of conduct, and as long as the employer is not using unethical practices or charging exorbitant interest rates—usury. Individual Christians must seek God's guidance and the leading of the Holy Spirit regarding their personal involvement in the practice of lending and borrowing.

David Wesley Whitlock serves as the Associate Provost, Dean of the College of Business and Computer Science, and Professor of Business Administration at Southwest Baptist University. He holds the BS and MBA from Southeastern Oklahoma State University, and the PhD from the University of Oklahoma.

Capital Rationing and the Fall

R. Barry Ellis

WHY DOES capital rationing exist? It is due to the fall of man and mankind's resulting sin nature. Why does top corporate management impose external capital budgeting constraints upon divisions before projects have been evaluated instead of telling the divisions to simply do all good projects and not to do any bad projects? Divisions and departments are given limited budgeting discretion due to the sin nature of mankind. Managers put their own interests ahead of those of owners. They violate the spirit of Peter's admonition, "Servants, be subject to your masters with all respect, not only to the good and gentle but also to the unjust" (1 Pet. 2:18 ESV).

If financial markets could trust management to only engage in positive net present value projects, corporations would always be able to raise funds for economically viable projects in an unfettered market. However, because markets cannot always trust corporate management, even firms desiring funds only for good projects face funding limitations. The resulting limitation in corporate funding leads to limits for divisional funding.

Additionally, top management recognizes the temptation for division heads to grow their divisions beyond optimal. Recognizing that the firm as a whole will not be able to optimize, they shoot for the best possible suboptimization by imposing capital budget constraints and asking each division to optimize within its budget constraint. Thus, the divergence between actual capital budget allocations and optimal capital budget allocations is one of the costs of our sin nature.

R. Barry Ellis is an Associate Professor of Finance at the University of Central Oklahoma. He holds the BBA from Baylor University, the MBA from East Texas State University and the PhD from the University of North Texas.

www.ingramcontent.com/pod-product-compliance
Lightning Source LLC
Chambersburg PA
CBHW060604230426
43670CB00011B/1956